BUSINESS BIG TIME

Secret Strategies to Explosively Grow Your Business Even If You Start Small

Dilim Okeke

Published By:

KEMCORP INNOVATIONS

www.dilimokeke.com

dilimokeke@gmail.com

+2348023871004, +2348092419056

All texts, calls, letters, testimonies and enquiries are welcome.

ENDORSEMENTS

...Breezy, captivating, informative, has depth

"Business Big Time is one great book you won't drop once you start reading, what with its breezy captivating prose; its informative irrefutable related local and global cases.

Dilim carries you along with her enthralling conversational style (a good one that purges you of that boredom, that tedium which comes with strictly intellectual texts), empowering you with an MBA- Marketing-dose-in-a-capsule.

In brief, Business Big Time has depth; it is a richly practical how-to-do-it entrepreneurial handbook that is not only a useful tool for aspiring entrepreneurs but for growing entrepreneurs as well as teachers and students of entrepreneurship."

\- **Siaka Momoh, Publisher/CEO The Real Sector.**

..Brilliant piece of work

"I have read quite some books on business in my time. Business Big Time is a brilliant piece of work and enormously helpful to any business – big or small – to generate greater profits even with minimal capital"

– Tolulope Aribisala. MD/CEO Krysolyte Bags

...Challenged my mindset

"Business Big Time is not your average business book. It is an interesting adventure that simplifies the increasingly tough entrepreneurial process with great insight and vivid applicable examples. Despite being an experienced entrepreneur with a few succeeding businesses, this book has challenged my mindset. You have to absolutely love failure to not succeed by reading this book."

– Kingsley Aigbona, Author - The Z of Marketing.

...Thoroughly researched and gives step-by-step direction for every stage your business is in

"Dilim covers it all! Her free conversational style sucks you in and allows any reader to see how it's possible to succeed in creating their own wealth.

Starting a business small and growing it big is obviously her passion. She knows her stuff and presents it in a way that is clear and straight to the point.

Her case studies are indepth and show a variety of people who started small and grew to become phenomenal. Most writers will stop at giving us successful case studies but Dilim went into practical details of how you too can apply these strategies for phenomenal success. One of the things I love most about this book is the fact that it is thoroughly researched and gives step-by-step direction for every stage your business is in.

"I suggest you have a notepad with you as you read this book or highlight passages that you need to read again and execute" Any savvy business person can be successful with this – Dilim reveals everything. Everything!!!"

– Ebuka Ewuzie. MD/CEO Bukasin Global Touch, and Author – The Secret Of Champions.

Dedication

To my husband: Thank you for supporting me all through.

To my awesome kids: Thank you for understanding why mummy had to work so many late nights.

To the loving memory of my father Augustine Ezeilo. I didn't have the opportunity to say goodbye to you. You always believed in me and taught me great entrepreneurial values. Thank you.

TABLE OF CONTENTS

Forward Quotes

"*Capital isn't so important in business. Experience isn't so important. You can get both of those things. What is important is ideas. If you have ideas, you have the main asset you need, and there isn't any limit to what you can do with your business and your life. They are any man's greatest assets – ideas.*" – **Harvey Firestone**

"*The critical ingredient is getting off your butt and doing something. It's as simple as that. A lot of people have ideas, but there are a few who decide to do something about them NOW. Not tomorrow, and not next week, but TODAY. The true entrepreneur is a doer, not a dreamer.*" – **Nolan Bushnell**

"In places where people see a lot of obstacles, I see a lot of opportunities...The entire world is a big market...."
– Orji Kalu

"Entrepreneurship is simply having the courage to just do it." **– Barbara Cash**

WHAT IS THIS BOOK ABOUT?

Before we get started, I'd like to introduce myself and let you know what this book is about. Just as important – what it's not about.

This book is not about teaching you the basics of starting a business of your own – yet the explosive growth strategies I am going to share with you will help you start out your business better guided for increased profits.

This book is not about any set formula for business success – yet these explosive growth strategies will help you exponentially grow your business fast.

This book is certainly not about handing you any specific business idea or "new" business niche, yet you are about to learn proven strategies that will help you create wealth faster with **your** own pre-conceived business ideas.

I know more than anyone that feeling that comes to you when you desire to start your own business. You are excited and fearful all at once. You've probably tested and validated your idea but have limited resources to begin with. In some cases, you have the capital but fear of the unknown "business territory" keeps you from making that crucial move.

I have also seen many businesses that have great potentials for growth remain mediocre. Often times because the owner lacks the vision to do so, but mainly because the owner lacks the right information on strategic ways to expand and gain traction fast.

This is not another methodical "stiff" textbook about how to start, finance and grow a business. Neither will you get a masterfully outlined and organized "how to write a business plan in this book". There are no theories in this book. Everything you will learn in this book is based on real-world experience. While some are from my own successful entrepreneurial journey so far in an economy like Nigeria's, some are insights I gained from my mentors (reputable mentors both within and outside Nigeria). Others still are thoroughly researched and proven strategies from grounded businesses from around the globe.

For example, when I first started out – after several years of graduation without any paid employment – I had very little capital (don't get me started on how tough it was for me to come up even with that little amount). So small was my capital that I knew for sure that I couldn't risk it on any untested business. For starters if I blew it, I knew there was none coming forth again – at least not anytime soon. Yet I didn't want to run your everyday conventional business. I wanted something a little different; something I could run both offline and online successfully. I also knew it had to be something I could run conveniently from home – my capital was so small that I had to minimize every overhead cost (if any at all).

I chose the hair growth and hair treatment product niche business. My research showed it to be a thriving business category – perhaps even slightly cluttered. I wanted my business to stand out so I chose to do something a little different from what others in the business in Nigeria were doing at the time. I decided to specialize purely on Indian herbal hair treatment products. The idea was to leverage on the word "Indian" (Indians are associated with long hair and effective herbal stuff).

But there was a little problem.

I needed to prove and be certain that my chosen niche was profitable and worth investing my precious capital in. I decided to conduct some form of test.

Back then, SMS marketing was still kind of novel and didn't get on peoples' nerves as much as it does now. I got myself a random list of about 3000 mobile telephone numbers scattered all over the country (I needed to find out if people would in any way at all respond to such an ad). So I typed up a somewhat cheesy message about growing long and beautiful hair with Indian herbal hair re-growth products and sent out to my random list.

Needless to say, the following minutes after I hit the send button on my laptop was fraught with nerves. I wasn't sure of what to expect. I held my breath and waited.

The result?

At first, the calls trickled in and then... my phone literarily rang off its hook that day. The price and other enquiries kept coming in even days after the SMS was sent. I really didn't count the calls that came in but getting anything between 100-150 price inquiries and pre-orders from a random list was more than enough for me to know I was right on target.

So how did I start my hair treatment products

business from home? More importantly, what strategies of growth did I take to capitalize on my newly discovered niche?

Or, how can small businesses operating on shoestring budgets grow fast? What fast, massive and comprehensive actions can they take to achieve explosive growth?

These strategies and how **you** can apply them to your new or existent business is what this book is about.

If you've got a business idea you'd like to establish and grow, or you already have an existing business but you feel stagnated and growth is a problem. You may think you need tons of capital to expand your business.

In my experience, after establishing several successful online and offline businesses from home, I have found that limited capital is rarely the only reason for business stagnation. Inability to strategize and utilize proven growth expansion tactics is more often the case.

This book will take you on a journey of how to take **your** business ideas to the market and make money with it. It will teach you how to readily duplicate your successes with your products and services in an economy like Nigeria's.

You will also learn how to quickly consolidate the successes you achieve and rapidly multiply it with minimal capital.

Once you understand the foundational basics of taking your own business ideas to the market for increased profits, you will be better equipped to exploit the many proliferating business opportunities that abound in a developing economy like Nigeria's.

That's what this book is about.

Throughout this book you will find some really useful tips; I call them Wealth Creation Nuggets. I have carefully segmented these nuggets to simplify different strategies. They do not appear in any particular order but you will find them really insightful and easy-to-recall when applying them to your own business.

Over the years, I have assembled actionable quotes that have helped me keep the zeal for success alive and to stay focused in business.

At the end of chapter 10 I have written out some of them for you as a bonus to help keep you on track. You can hurriedly go through them when you need fast motivation. Or you can print them out and tape it somewhere within sight for easy access.

Let's get started!

CHAPTER 1: **WHY BUSINESS?**

"He who has a why can endure any how." - Friedrich Nietzsche

Quoting figures from the National Bureau of Statistics (NBS); No fewer than 5.3 million Nigerian youths are jobless, while 1.8 million graduates enter the labour market every year. From the same source, statistics show that about 20.3 million Nigerians are jobless! I'll have you know that these statistics totally excludes the tens of thousands that get laid off work every year. And oh, it doesn't even begin to account for the several million youths who were not fortunate enough to attend a higher institution or to acquire some basic skills roaming the streets of the country as touts and common labourers!

Sure, you could wait for the government to create more job openings and have at least 1000 people apply for the same post. If you're lucky, you just might beat the 1000:1 probability stakes and secure the job (seriously, this is unlikely), or you could fold your arms, lament all day long on the troubled economy and wait for some visionary and hard working entrepreneur to set up a business and employ you in his business as his bean counter!

I am not against salaried jobs. No, that is not the purpose of this book. I simply find it totally upsetting seeing people with great potentials submit application after application, suffer rejection after rejection, and they repeat this pattern year after year until the first signs of grey begin to show on their head. How sad!

Let's face it; it's downright difficult to get a well-paying and steady job now in the present economy and the deepening recession. Besides, advanced machinery and computers are fast replacing human labour in almost every sector of employment. On the other hand, a business of your own has the potential for growth and can generate a lot more income and wealth for you.

WEALTH CREATION NUGGET

Fear breeds excuses. Let go of your
fear – or it will cripple you.

Sure, I understand that the fear of failure amongst other

vague reasons has kept many prospective business owners from starting a business of their own. Of course, any business can fail but with the right attitude and proper planning, every business has potentials for growth.

WEALTH CREATION NUGGET

No matter your background, education, profession or even the life experiences you gathered over the years, you've probably had a few ideas for business.

Everyone has at one time or the other had an idea for one business or another. The problem is that most people give up on their business ideas too soon for various – often times – intangible reasons. In my experience, I have found that many business ideas could be valid and simpler (to execute) than you realize without requiring enormous outlays of cash; just good old-fashioned dedication and effort.

I totally agree with business establishment experts that the major investment in most self-owned businesses and start-ups is an investment of one's self in the form of time, focus and persistence.

If you belong to the class of people who have allowed themselves be crippled by fear and doubts; this is probably not a book for you.... or perhaps, it's just the wake-up call you need to finally begin to explore the entrepreneur within you! You decide.

WEALTH CREATION NUGGET

Don't wait until you can start out "perfect" – but you need to start out "defined".

While many people are afraid to start a business because of fear of failure and perceived lack of adequate resources, the majority of the people that do start a business are really not clear on why they want to or should start their own business.

Let's face it, entrepreneurship is not for everyone. Starting and managing your own business is not child's play. It takes a lot of effort, it takes motivation, drive, desire, skills, talents, time – and of course, resources. It also takes careful research and planning. Just like in a game of chess (not one of my favourite games though!), success in your business starts with decisive and correct opening moves.

If you choose the path of entrepreneurship, you must be committed to it and you should be every bit sure you are starting your business for the right reasons.

CRUCIAL QUESTION: AM I PREPARED FOR ENTREPRENEURSHIP?

Every serious entrepreneur knows that starting a business from scratch can be as intimidating as it is rewarding. Nevertheless, it is important to understand what this might mean for you. Before you invest time and money into getting your business off the ground, I recommend that you really get honest with yourself. You might find it helpful to determine your own entrepreneurial strengths and weaknesses.

I have created an entrepreneurial quiz below to help you. Answer yes or no:

- I am willing to learn.

- I have determination

- I have a passion for success and achievement.

- I have a zeal for the tasks ahead.

- I have a positive attitude.

- My personality is flexible

- I am a confident person

- I have the ability to focus

- I like to problem solve

- I see possibilities where others see problems

- I am open to new ways of doing things

- I can make sacrifices in the short-term for long-term rewards

- I like to be in control

- I am willing to take (calculated) risks

- I take responsibility for my own actions

- I learn from mistakes

- I am emotionally strong

- I can connect with others and build strategic relationships

- I can adapt to changing environment and times

- I am curious and continually in search of discovery

- I can hang on in bad times and recover quickly

- I feel comfortable making important decisions

If you answered yes to all these questions, then you are one super-hot-entrepreneurial-genius-bombshell and the world is awaiting your announcement!

Frankly, there really is no definitive right or wrong answer to these questions, but there are certain attributes that are closely associated with success in any kind of business. If you're truly passionate about starting and growing your own business, you need to know and build on your strengths while improving steadfastly on your weaknesses.

BEFORE GETTING STARTED

Your "why" is what inspires you, gives direction, sparks action, and breathes life into everything you do. Before starting out, identify your reasons for wanting to establish a business.

Many people establish a business only to just "go with the flow". Starting a business with no clear directions for what you want and hope to achieve is often a recipe for failure. Lack of direction and focus has killed off many businesses than you can imagine. Understanding and clearly defining what you hope to achieve by starting a business is probably one of the most empowering steps you can take for a successful entrepreneurial journey because your personal purpose will drive your performance as a founder.

I have listed some of the most common reasons you ought to and should consider starting and owning a business of your own.

- I am unemployed

- I have just been laid off work

- I want to be my own boss

- I want financial freedom

- I am employed but underpaid

- I have just identified a major untapped market (don't we all want this?)

- I want to fully use my skills and knowledge

- I have a unique and marketable idea

- I want to make my millions (Yay!)

Next, you need to determine what type of business is

right for you.

- What do I like to do with my time?

- What skills – technical or otherwise – have I learnt or developed?

- What do others say I am good at?

- How much time do I have to run a successful business?

- Do I have any hobbies or interests that are marketable?

- What marketable and duplicable experiences have I got?

You know sometimes the answers to these questions are just right in front of you. Sometimes you may need to scratch a little deeper to find them. I have seen people who have marketable talents take these talents for granted and go searching for their "golden fleece" under hard rocks.

Many times, many aspiring entrepreneurs start a

business they are not naturally poised to exploit. You'll find that starting a business simply because it is promoted as the next shiny object or because your neighbour is in the same type business and he just acquired a new mansion often leads to failure and frustration.

For example, the fact that popular Nigerian blogger Linda Ikeji of lindaikejisblog.com has built a highly profitable blogging business has made many young (and not so young) Nigerians decide to go into the celebrity/news/gossip blogging business. If you have the knack and skills for blogging like Linda, then by all means start a blogging business and knock out your competitors while you're at it! But, if you do not read about nor follow celebrity gossip, you are an absolute introvert with little social life and you would rather spend your free time reading and watching scientific documentaries. Heck, you don't even have a social profile on any of the many social media and the name Kim K totally irks you; what business could you possibly have blogging about celebrities and their social – and not so social life?

For me, deciding on what business was right for me was really straightforward. I love selling. I grew up buying and re-selling alongside my parents (remember what I wrote earlier about the experiences you've gathered? They have a way of influencing what you do). I always loved the world of buying and reselling even when I was in the university. It really didn't matter one bit what saleable item I bought and resold as long as I had designed and perfected ways to sell it fast and profitably too. I simply thrive on making smart negotiations and closing sales quickly.

While I love the busy and unpredictable world of buying and reselling for a profit, some are solely interested in the manufacturing side of business, and others prefer the less chaotic world of the service industry and so on.

Use the criteria above to identify what category of business would suit you (I will discuss specifics later in this chapter). The reality is that you are better poised for success in your business when you love what you are doing. Frustration often sets in when you are trying to make money in a business you know little or nothing about and probably loathe.

You should also identify the target market your business will serve. It is counter-productive to try to serve everyone all at once. Conduct necessary research to answer these questions:

- Is my idea practical and will it fill a need?
- Every single business has competition, so, what is my competition?
- What is my business advantage over existing similar businesses?
- Can I create better quality service or products?
- Can I create demand for my products and/or services?

The final step before fully developing your business concept is what I call the Pre-Business Checklist. This time, you need to be specific with your answers.

- What specific business am I interested in starting?
- What services or products will I sell?
- Where will I be located? Will it be online, offline or both?

- What skills and experiences do I bring to the table?

- What (strategic) name will I give my business?

- What financing will I need?

- What are my immediately and/or easily accessible resources?

- How far can I get with my immediately and/or easily accessible resources before my business requires a new inflow of resources?

Your answers to the Pre-Business Checklist deals with specifics that will help you create a focused and balanced plan before you begin.

Yes, I do expect you to research and test your idea before fully embarking on it, but I do not suggest that you spend an eternity (and lots of limited funds perhaps) seeking to "perfect" your plan – the business world doesn't work that way. In reality, the business world is often spontaneous and filled with risks, but even that is based on some form of well researched and structured plan.

Needless to say, there really isn't one success-proof and rigid set of rules and guidelines that ultimately guarantees success in any business.

Success in business is really more of a complex yet rewarding process of gathering pieces of information from here, combining various ideas from there, getting this right, goofing that up, and generally adapting together all you know (or learnt) until you find that right combination that works perfectly for your specific type of business.

Whatever your reasons for wanting to start a business might be, no doubt you have the potential to generate a lot more wealth but, you'd better be prepared to put on hold your "happy go lucky" life and be ready to put in some ample lot of hard and smart work.

Perhaps, I should re-title this chapter "Why Not Business"? It's time for you to explore the entrepreneur within you – who knows where it might lead you?

CHAPTER 2: **DEVELOPING A WINNING MINDSET- WHEN WINNING IS ALL THAT MATTERS**

"The winners in life think constantly in terms of I can, I will, and I am" - Dennis Waitley

I'll make this chapter a quick read. An entrepreneur with a winners' mindset has a non-negotiable goal of success – Period!

Do you know your thoughts are the only things you have 100% control over? It is true. It is also true that "battles are won and lost in peoples' head long before they are fought". One critical battle in your quest for success as an entrepreneur is that of the level of your self-confidence. You either win it or lose it first in your head – and it all starts with your mindset.

FLOW CHART HERE

Beliefs Thoughts Actions Results (in the middle mindset)

The one thing people tend to forget is that thoughts are not random; you can learn to control them.

Choosing to learn how to control your thought patterns will correct your mindset and ensure that you always perform with an aura of self-belief and confidence.

WINNER OR LOSER?

Okay, let's try to understand what a winning mindset is: a winning mindset is believing that no matter what challenges come your way (be sure they will – loads of it too!), you will keep getting off the ground and continue to move forward till the finish line is in front of you – and you cross it. Put simply, the winning mindset will do even that which is deemed impossible to achieve its goal of success.

As an entrepreneur, a crucial key to your growth and success is to develop a winning mindset. There will be times when you are feeling completely overwhelmed. Times when it feels as if the universe itself is against all your efforts and frustration makes you want to throw in the towel in defeat. At such times, an unrelenting winning mindset keeps you looking for and developing ways to growth.

Your mindset dictates your moods, your emotions, your actions, and ultimately your ability to perform. With a winners' mindset, you are not starting your business "to try". You are starting your business with every sense of assurance.

Several factors influence your success as an entrepreneur; some of them are obvious, like money, skills, and talents. Others are less obvious. An undervalued yet most powerful trait of every successful business owner is self-confidence.

The old man in the story below lost his.

HOW STRONG IS YOUR BELIEF?

Your ability to keep and maintain a positive mental attitude is of utmost importance in every business. This is true for most start-ups. In simple words; your level of belief is major and critical to your success.

There was once an old man who was both an illiterate and hard of hearing - but he made great suya. He would stand by the side of the road with his suya stand and sell his hot and spicy suya. His suya was very tasteful and customers thronged his suya stand.

One day, his son – he'd earned enough money to send the young man away to school – came home from the university and said to his father, "Don't you know how bad the economy is? Everyone is starving, being laid off work, going bankrupt and no one has extra to spend on suya".

The old man thought "My son must know. He can read and write. He's gone to school. If he says times are hard, then he must be correct. So he took down his suya stand sign. He cut back on the meat and exotic choice spices he was known for, and he stopped going out beside the road every day.

Guess what happened? His tasteless and lacklustre suya made him lose most of his customers. Just as he had believed, his business declined and kept declining until he could no longer support himself. Finally, he was forced to close down.

And the old man said to himself, "My son was right. The economy is so bad; no one would want to spend money on suya in times like these."

Over and over again, I have seen people lock themselves into a "loser or victim" mindset that just makes everything happen in the way they DON'T want it to happen... BUT, that they had expected it to happen from the very beginning. How ironic! You need to understand that ensuring the way you approach your new start-up or existing business is mentally correct is a major key to success because, your attitude, beliefs, thoughts and words actually affect what you experience as a reality.

A winning mindset is a state of mind; and not a feeling that lasts only for a moment(s). It also isn't a wish or a desire. It goes beyond the scope of your knowledge and is not about trusting alone in your capabilities. A winning mindset is actually a result of your self-confidence that is there even before the results of your actions. In one word, it is FAITH.

I can't stress mindset enough. I don't want you to confuse a winning mindset with wishful positive thinking or wishful "positive confession". If you do that then you would be living in a mere fantasy world. And the last time I checked; fantasies and daydreams do not pay the bills.

CHAMPIONS FAIL FORWARD

So you failed in the past or probably did not leave college with the best grades, or perhaps, you did not even go to college at all. Worse still, your case is that of a failed business and you lost some of your investments?

Sorry about your loss, but – so what? You can choose to wallow away in self-pity, sulking and readily giving excuses, or, you can choose to dust yourself up, brace up, learn from your mistakes, adjust and march on! That's what champions do.

Think about it: some of the world's most successful people failed at first – sometimes more than once. Thomas Edison's teachers told him he was "too stupid to learn anything". Billionaire Warren Buffet wasn't accepted at Harvard University because he "wasn't smart enough". Walt Disney was fired by a newspaper editor because he "lacked imagination" and "had no good ideas". Oprah Winfrey was fired from her first television job but she rebounded and became the undisputed "American queen of television talk show". Not only that, she also became the first billionaire woman of the African-American descent. Nigeria's own billionaire Mike Adenuga was at a time a taxi driver and Orji Kalu was rusticated from the university . . . and the list goes on.

You must realize that not everyone who's on top today got there with success after success. More often than not, these winners we celebrate their successes today went through the toughest periods before they made it big.

It's normal to fail; winners remain that way not because they never failed but because they know that failure isn't the end but a learning process. The idea is not to avoid failure by doing nothing, but for you to move out of your comfort zone, eliminating obstacle after obstacle, until you get what you really want and attain your life goals.

I won't even begin to attempt teaching you how to develop a winning mindset in this book – several books are written by experts for that purpose already. Instead, I will let you into some common characteristics of successful entrepreneurs with the winning mindset.

A successful entrepreneur with a winning mindset:

- Sets clear goals for his life and business
- Has a focused mind and keeps his eyes on the progress towards each goal
- Constantly takes actions that are in harmony with his visions
- Is open to opportunities that will enhance the value of his business

- Studies and evaluates every business decision with respect to his objectives

- He takes full responsibility for all his actions and decisions

- He learns from his mistakes as well as successes

- He never stops learning

- He looks for the lesson or opportunity in every problem and pivots it into a favourable situation

Being a winner in life isn't a one-time thing. It's a series of habits that will eventually make you a consistent person in every endeavour you face. Winning is an ongoing process as you continue to increase your experience and take on different challenges.

A winning mindset may not be the guarantee to your business being successful: but it sure is a huge and major landmark on your success journey. Ultra success in business comes to those who seek it and refuse to accept anything less. Bottom-line: it all starts with you .

.. and the sort of mindset you permit to grow in you.

CHAPTER 3: **HOW SMALL IS YOUR CAPITAL ANYWAY?**

"Capital can do nothing without brains

to direct it" - J. Ogden Armour

SUBJECT: I Have 2 Million Naira, What Profitable Business Can I Do?

BODY: *"Please house, I need your sincere advice on a good business I can start with 2 million naira that's not so stressful but profitable. I am in my late 20's, so I am not getting younger anymore. I, therefore, think it's time to start up something that will help to give the kind of future I desire. Thanks"*

SUBJECT: *What Kind Of Business Will Someone Start With N500,000 In Nigeria?*

BODY: *Fellow Nairalander, I need your contributions on any business one can start with 500,000 naira in Nigeria instead of depositing the said amount in a bank. Your contributions will be much appreciated.*

SUBJECT: *I Have 52,000 Naira. What Business Do I Start?*

BODY: *Hi Pals. I am a graduate with the sum of 52,000 naira only. I don't know any profitable business right now in Nigeria. If any of you has great ideas, please help me.*

I lifted these requests for business ideas from nairaland.com – arguably Nigeria's most popular online discussion forum. A casual browse through Nairaland's business list will reveal more requests such as these – and the much more seriously unnerving solutions being proffered! Seriously, I don't know which I find more unsettling between the requests for business ideas on a public platform or the sometimes totally preposterous solutions posted! Oh, well!

Apparently, a lot of people ranging from the enterprising undergraduate, the unemployed, the retired and even the employed-but-far-from-financially-secured-employee would like to be financially independent. Most would like to start a business of their own, but don't because of perceived lack of adequate funds and shortage of business ideas (By the way-I made it clear that this is NOT a book on business ideas)

From the posts above, you will notice that "small" and "big" capital is relative. While one considers 2 million naira too small to start a suitable business, another would go give a thanksgiving in the church if he could only get started with 52,000 naira only! Frankly, "It takes money to make money" but on the other hand, starting a business with a fat bank account is not a guarantee for success either.

Dig deep and conduct a little research, you will find that for about every 1000 businesses established as start-ups, about 900 of it failed; or at best, remained mediocre. Take your research further and you will find that for the remaining successful 100 businesses, about 90 of them started on shoestring budgets; in other words "small capital"- before growing them into the big businesses they are today.

My point is, as much as starting a business well funded from the beginning is beneficial, it doesn't necessarily guarantee that your start-up business will be successful. What does guarantee your success is actually much simpler – a combination of *your* ideas (well researched) + *your* guts + *your* creative persistence + *your* determination to see things through. Now, this is one age-long formula that is constantly reproduced and duplicated in every successful business you and I know and celebrate today.

So what if you have to start from your home, in your garage, in your basement, or even from your kitchen table? So what if you have to start with the funds presently available to you?

AMY'S KITCHEN: From Home-Based to Multi-Million Frozen Food Business

Long before organic food became a leading trend, Californian couple Andy and Rachel Berliner was into healthy eating and committed to a healthy vegetarian lifestyle.

At some point, when Rachel pulled a muscle and couldn't stand long enough to cook, husband Andy rushed to the local health food store to buy frozen dinners. What they discovered about frozen foods changed their lives ... and started them off into a highly successful entrepreneurial journey.

How Amy's Kitchen Started

Like many families who may not always have the energy or time to cook, Andy bought frozen dinners for his family. It was at a time when not many frozen meals are being offered for vegetarians. Andy bought several frozen meals, and the verdict was always the same: the frozen food tasted horrible. The food tasted like cardboard.

WEALTH CREATION NUGGET

See something missing? Maybe you are not the only one... A gap in the marketplace reveals a business opportunity.

Andy having previously run an organic tea company that he sold earlier saw the big potential of their discovery. They had found an under-served niche of this market poised to grow significantly in the next few years. They knew that there was a big market of consumers who wanted a convenient meal but still wanted to eat healthy, tasty and organic foods.

The couple believed that there was a big opportunity for a new entrant that would offer the one thing that the current players in the market were not offering: TASTE

It didn't take long for them to decide they would be that entrant. They would build their frozen food on health AND taste.

WEALTH CREATION NUGGET

"Don't try to serve everyone in your market. Carefully select and serve a reachable target within your market."

Their goal wasn't to appeal to the typical TV dinner eater or bachelor eater; it was to win over people who normally prepare their own healthy meals but occasionally don't have time to cook. They decided to name their business Amy's Kitchen, after their newborn daughter.

It All Began With A Humble Pot Pie

With pot pies being one of the most popular frozen meals, the Berliners decide to create their first product that will blow all other frozen potpies in terms of taste. With the help of Rachel's mum, Eleanor, they tested and tasted various products until they came up with a winning vegetable and tofu recipe.

The business was a family affair, with Andy doing the overall strategizing and dealing, Rachel designing product packaging and Eleanor creating the right mix of the vegetables. To market the business, the couple (and even Rachel's father) travelled the country to attend regional health food trade shows and made sales calls to food distributors. Gradually, their pot pies made its way from being homemade, to making a debut in health food shows and national health food stores. The response was great, with several natural food stores signing up for orders. And then came in the big stud in their wheels... the local organic bakery they approached to help them produce their products couldn't keep up with the orders anymore!

WEALTH CREATION NUGGET

Refuse to back down in the face of challenges; instead, TURN your challenges into avenues for growth

---

That forced Andy to take over production itself, a

process that he never envisioned he'd take on. Despite some steep learning curves and imaginative stretching of their limited budget, taking on the production itself allowed them to control the quality of their products and not compromise on food ingredients.

Since then Amy's has gone on to create over 250 frozen meals and has included a successful grocery line of products.

Amy's Kitchen products are presently carried by all natural food stores in the USA including big chains such as Kroger, SafeWay and Whole Foods.

I would like for you to note that Amy's Kitchen didn't start operations with millions in their account. No, it started on a shoestring budget. Andy sold his gold watch and gold coins, borrowed from relatives, and took a loan using Rachel's car as collateral; in other words, the Berliners started with only the funds that were immediately accessible to them. Their visionary and gutsy investment paid off.

The business that the Berliners started in their kitchen and operated out of their barn has grown into a multi-million dollar business with revenues in excess of $300 million and over 1500 employees..... And it all started with a humble potpie!

WEALTH CREATION NUGGET

CREATIVE ADAPTABILITY: Take a proven system that works for another business and/or geographical location and creatively tweak it to suit your specific needs for huge business breakthroughs.

Let me guess; you are probably thinking "Get real, how can a system that worked in developed USA be of any help to us here in Nigeria?" If that's your thought pattern, then I've got just one answer for you-"Get rid of your myopic vision! It has no place in business." The answer isn't in the geographical region and neither is it on the dates and time. The answer is in the principles employed which can be duplicated by anyone, anytime, anywhere and in any business.

For example, in the fashion industry, there really are no new styles. Top designers keep recreating and revamping "supposed" old and outdated styles in combination with the present fashion trend to create a newer look. They creatively tweak them only slightly and voila - a new vogue is born. In the same way, there really aren't "new", "revolutionary" strategies for growth. As a matter of fact, even if you stumbled on a totally new growth strategy, it probably wouldn't do you much good as a start-up. You'd probably have to spend more time and funds (which are limited-remember?) to test it and prove its usefulness. Unless you have a lot of time and funds to spare for testing, unproven strategies could actually end up being a burden to start-ups. Your best bet when starting on a shoestring budget or seeking for growth is to adapt proven strategies and recreate them for your own unique business needs.

I must reiterate here that if you do not yet realize that geographical location is often not a barrier to success in business, then I will refer you back to Chapter 2 of this book: Creating A Winning Mindset For Business.

But, if you are still hung on nailing me for bringing in an example of a small business turned big success story from developed countries, I will share with you the success story of the unknown but dedicated Austin brothers.

EXPLOITING YOUR EXPERIENCES FOR BREAKTHROUGH

Once there were no fast food eateries in Nigeria but only local food joints. Once there was only Mr. Biggs fast food eatery, but now the list is endless... and once, there were no ready-to-wear traditional garments.

GRAY KLOTTING

In the ancient city of Ibadan, the Austin brothers started their clothing business as young school undergraduates only as a part-time business. Growing up, they had watched and assisted their parents, trade on fabrics (commonly referred to as cut-and-sew) to make a living. It was the family business. In the early 2000's, cut-and-sew fabrics gave way to imported ready-to-wear garments and gradually, it was almost completely phased out. The "cut and sew" business soon went downhill and their parents closed shop and changed their line of business.

Running the business alongside their parents and older siblings had taught and given them some level of independence and experience. Several years later after several unsuccessful attempts at gaining admission into the university, the boys decided they could revive and still sell the "cut-and-sew" fabrics – all they needed to do was to take it a notch or two further.

They figured they could still access and sell to the same customer base but this time, they would approach the business with a twist. They would give their customers what they missed from "cut and sew" fabrics

but couldn't readily get from ready-to-wear garments –
high-quality fabrics custom made to your fit delivered
right to your doorstep and on time too! In essence, the
Austin brothers were selling four things:

- Quality and hard to find fabrics (especially in ready-to-wear garments)
- Custom-made exactly to your fit and taste
- Specialty and uniqueness
- Time: they saved their clients time to go shopping by hand-picking the fabrics and ensuring delivery

WEALTH CREATION NUGGET

*Picking a market you are
EXPERIENCED to exploit first and
then going after salable products is a
smart approach.*

Although the Austin Brothers had good experience in

hand-picking excellent quality fabrics, they had absolutely ZERO experience in sewing. They assembled tailors and seamstresses with excellent sewing skills but with little recognition of their own skills. Next, they followed leading fashion trends and armed themselves with reputable fashion catalogues. They paid attention to details by getting high-quality packaging materials at par with the imported garments packaging for their finished products.

Their key attractions are a distinctive touch of African details to their contemporary origin designs and distinctive Western details to their African origin designs. And thus, a clothing line was born – GRAY KLOTTING.

Gray Klotting marketed its products first to friends and family. Their first products were instant hits. People loved it and gradually spread the word. Although they had initially targeted Nigerian based consumers, Gray Klotting started getting international orders from Africans in the Diaspora when they went online with their products.

WEALTH CREATION NUGGET

Whenever possible, start quickly, start smartly and start affordably – And most of the time, it is possible

---

The important thing to note here is that the Austin Brothers created Gray Klotting with zero capital – they would collect a down payment and source their materials with the down payment and then collect the balance upon completion. They had no fixed overhead or payment of store lease, no employees and certainly, no recurring overhead costs. Their "office" was right in their parents' house and their assembly of tailors and seamstresses made the specified clothes in their own workshops under close supervision for a pre-agreed fee! Also very important; they custom-made their products only on demand.

Gray Klotting has positioned itself for growth and is definitely on a steady growth curve. The major constraint they have as at the time of writing this book is that, all three of the brothers are in different states in Nigeria as corp members with the NYSC (almost forgot – all 3 of them got admitted into the University shortly after they started their business) and have to shuttle between their station and work.

Recently, I asked one of the Austin brothers if he would leave Gray Klotting business for a salaried job upon graduation. I remember the smirk on his face as he answered "No, I love what I am doing. Besides, I see a lot of potentials for growth". I'll tell you what; even I see a strong growth potential for their business. With such vision and diligent work, Gray Klotting could very well become a celebrated multi-million naira business in the near future!

So, are you still worried about starting with a "small" capital? Look for ways to start with what you have. Cut costs where possible – not the quality of products or service – just avoidable costs.

Sometimes the appeal of appearing as a "big business" long before we achieve that status has been the undoing of many small businesses. I once watched a young woman who went around from family to friends to raise capital to start a business fizzle it all off unnecessarily.

She got handouts and loans from them but what did she do with it? First, she got a fancy shop, paid rent for 2 years, and went about "decorating" the shop. By the time she was done decorating, she barely had enough to fully stock her store – height of ineptitude I'd say. Her store was partially empty and poorly run. Needless to say, she ran herself out of business long before she could actually start.

The allure of "I have arrived" in business has been and still is the downfall of many small and medium-sized businesses. You'd be wise to avoid it at the early stage of your business –especially when your budget is limited – and focus on what matters which is growing your business.

CHAPTER 4: **EXPLOSIVE GROWTH STRATEGY #1: CREATE PRODUCT FROM SCRATCH FOR ENORMOUS BREAKTHROUGHS**

" I do not think there is any thrill that can go through the human heart like that felt by the inventor as he sees some creation of the brain unfolding to success . . . such emotions make a man forget food, sleep, friends, love, everything." **- Nikola Tesla**

Start counting all the products – in other words, other people's invention – you see from the very moment you wake up every morning. Count your alarm clock, bed sheets, toothpaste, toothbrush, refrigerator, beverages, sanitary wares, toilet paper, mobile phones, television, computer, shoes, pen, car... you get the picture. All of these and more are other people's inventions that made life easier for humanity and made their inventors millions... heck, even billions!

Truthfully, the word invention can be intimidating but you would be surprised by the ample number of Nigerians with brilliant invention ideas but do not validate their ideas let alone working their ideas out. Some don't go far with their ideas because of sheer laziness and sometimes, a morbid fear of failure. Worse still, others do not let their invention ideas go beyond their beautiful imaginations because of their weak (in my opinion) perception of the "Nigerian environment" (remember Winning Mindset?).

I am not even in the slightest campaigning that you invest all your hard earned money and time attempting to be another Thomas Edison or Henry Ford (having a Nigerian Ford and Edison would be great, though!). My mission here is to open our eyes to the many simple but relevant inventions that have made their inventors super wealthy over time. The most successful inventions are those that proffer simple, yet effective solutions to human needs.

SO YOU'VE GOT A BRILLIANT IDEA – NOW WHAT?

If your sole reason for wanting to invent a product from scratch is to make millions right away, don't hold your breath! Making millions, perhaps even billions is not impossible with your brilliant ideas, BUT, the harsh reality is that brilliant ideas are just those... ideas... until you turn them into saleable products.

WEALTH CREATION NUGGET

Get in front and lead a crowd of people who are already marching; not to get a crowd of people to start marching.

Other than the short-lived ecstatic value, there's no value to an invention that will not succeed in the market – period! Just because you spent all your life's earnings and valuable time creating the product doesn't mean people will flock to buy it. No. People will only buy products that they need. Therefore, before going ahead and putting in the effort, you must make sure your invention has market potential. Here, my very best business advice to you is to create a product only if you know how you will market it and that you can market it for profits. In simple words, WORK BACKWARDS in 4 steps:

- Be sure there's an existent market for related product categories

- Determine effective marketing strategies to reach the market

- Be sure the market is affordably accessible and reachable

- Invent to suit the market needs

HOW A "SILLY" PRODUCT CONCEPT MADE ITS OWNER A MILLIONAIRE.... MANY TIMES OVER.

For every Bill Gates (Microsoft) and Mark Zuckerberg (Facebook), there are thousands of inventors who are hardly popular, but still quietly make fortunes from their inventions. I could write about these globally recognized inventors, but I choose to write about Nancy Jarecki – a woman entrepreneur who "accidentally" discovered a silent market opportunity, went for it, made it a reality, and today is reaping in millions in sales. Her story is full of wealth creation strategies that even you could make use of.

SUCCESS WITH AN UNCONVENTIONAL BEAUTY PRODUCT

Nancy Jarecki was in a hair salon while vacationing in Rome. She noticed that some women after having their hair coloured would linger at the door apparently waiting for something. After a few minutes, their hair colourist would come back with a little paper bag, hand it to them and send them cheerfully on their way. Asking one of the colorists, she learned that the women were waiting to get a hair colouring kits so their hair "down there" can match their new hair colour.

WEALTH CREATION NUGGET

It is incredibly important to have your opportunity "antennae" up at all times

---

She discovered that women everywhere get so frustrated with mismatched hair colours in their bodies. Blondes want to be true blondes and have their hair down there spot the same shade, and so do red heads and other colours.

It was also a convenient concealer for the unsightly grays for the hair "down there".

She plunged into action and made enquiries from several Gynecologists about how many women match – more than half don't. With her opportunity antennae up, Nancy realized she had just uncovered an untapped market.

She immediately assembled some chemists and dermatologists to work out a formula for a dye that was both mild and gentle on the skin. Her products "For The Hair Down There" launched successfully into the market and received great acceptance with many women (and men too! Who would have guessed?) happily matching their hair colour down there!

WEALTH CREATION NUGGET

Create a business with backend growth options – a business with potential for long-term relationship with customers providing related products and services

---

Does her idea sound insane? Well, apparently not so. Nancy Betty's company has brought in multi-million in sales and she keeps coming up with new products to serve her niche market.

Nancy provided a simple solution to a silent need of many women and men (still trying to get over this!) All she did was proper research of the existent hair dye market and a little tweaking of the already existent hair dye products and she was home free – smiling all the way to the bank. In her own words, "I hadn't planned on starting a cosmetics company". The success of it all lies in the fact the market was already existing, known, identified and affordably reachable –and fortunately for her, untapped.

If it appears that people are clamouring to have a solution to some problem and that solution appears to be your invention, then you have a great chance of marketing your invention successfully.

FROM A DOOR-TO-DOOR SALES WOMAN TO BECOMING "WORLD'S SELF-MADE YOUNGEST FEMALE BILLIONAIRE

Sara Blakely had been selling fax machines and office copiers door-to-door for seven years when she came up with the idea for Spanx. Spanx body shapers are body shaping undergarments designed to give a smooth and toned appearance to a woman's figure. These body shapers are designed to be invisible under clothing, providing "smooth support" and "target shaping" while at the same time eliminating unsightly visible panty lines.

THE STORY OF SPANX

In Sara's own words, *"I did not like the way I looked in a new pair of white pants (ladies trousers) I had just bought. I was 27 at the time and had spent a lot of money on them, but you could see the panty lines and you could also see the thong. I tried every available undergarment to hide the visible panty lines but nothing worked. I shopped for body shapers for the first time in my life and I was horrified. They were thick – it was like wearing work-out clothes and they* all had a leg band on one side that showed through the

pants. So I cut the feet off of a pantyhose and it allowed

me to wear a pair of great strappy sandals. I didn't see

lines anymore but the hose rolled-up my feet ... and

that's how Spanx was born."

WEALTH CREATION NUGGET

*How often have you been frustrated
using a product and thought you could
do better? Turn your frustrations into
avenues for huge profits*

Imagine having recently bought a piece of expensive

clothing with your meager income and not being able to

wear it and show it off? Of course, Sara was frustrated

with the limited options available! A simple experiment

she carried out of her frustration gave birth to Spanx-now a mega business empire.

You will notice that Sara's Spanx "invention" was simply genius – but not entirely new. Her *Aha*! moment of inspiration came when she tried on the existent body shapers – they appeared body slimming but too thick and uncomfortable; the pantyhose with cut-off feet – they were light textured and hid panty lines perfectly but they rolled and bunched up uncomfortably up her legs. Instantly she realized that a cross combination of an undergarment that was butt firming, comfortably light textured, designed to hide panty lines and to stay above the knees without bunching up was what every woman would want—and more importantly, gladly *pay* for.

From Spanx idea conception to realization was quite a journey. She had little capital to start with and her idea was rejected by many manufacturers who thought her idea was "dumb". Sara believed firmly in her idea and guts and pressed on, and the rest is ....well, the world's youngest female self-made billionaire.

How often have you bought a product or been rendered a service that you thought was poor? How often have you been so dismayed at the level of quality and you thought to yourself "Even I can do better than that"? Better still, how often have you been able to provide a quick and effective solution to a nagging problem and thought nothing of it? Sara is no different than most of us. The major difference is that in her case, she recognized it as an untapped opportunity and acted fast on commoditizing a simple but effective solution.

What both Nancy and Sara's story have in common – aside from the millions and billions of course – is providing simple solutions to every day yet overlooked problems.

WEALTH CREATION NUGGET

Provide simple solutions

THE INVENTION FATAL FLAW TO AVOID

"I had a great idea", "I think it will be really good", "I'm really good at this", "I am really interested in this", "I've always loved this ever since I was a kid", "I checked with a few friends and they also think it's a great idea", "My husband/wife thinks it's a nice idea" ... see a pattern here? Well, this pattern is a totally flawed logic to base your invention upon. So many inventions created based on flawed sentiments have failed because it lacked relevance in the real world.

Creating a product from scratch is not about what you want, like, need or think is right. It is about providing a solution to an identified, measurable and ***easily accessible*** market with a want, like or need.

I would advise that in creating a new product, you shouldn't try to completely re-invent the wheel—or try so hard to make it so unique that it doesn't fit into any pre-established categories.

If you are determined that the business of your choice is to be a product inventor, I would encourage you to invest in one or two well-regarded books on invention. Look for those that focus both on how to successfully take your completed invention to the market and on how to make money with your product.

You must also learn how to protect your idea and even

if your idea is worth protecting. You must decide if you want to manufacture your products or if you will license your ideas to a manufacturer—in Nigeria or overseas.

You must decide if you will be taking your product invention to the market yourself or if you would rather supply existent distribution chains.

You simply have to be an avid student and the internet is filled with useful resources that can help you.

The product invention route is a tough one but totally worth it when your product becomes a market success. Who knows? Perhaps the next great invention would be from Nigeria – and it just could be yours.

CHAPTER 5: EXPLOSIVE GROWTH STRATEGY #2: How Exclusive Rights Ownership Can Make You Millions

---

"Wealth creation is most often linked to the exclusive ownership of a particular concept, product or service" - Dilim Okeke

---

One of the hidden secrets of explosively growing your small business is doing everything within your power to eliminate circumstances beyond your control.

Exclusive rights mean no one else can purchase or sell that product without purchasing through you, including wholesalers, distributors, affiliates and retailers. In other words, when you have exclusive rights to another persons' products, you own that product even though you are not manufacturing it, bear zero manufacturing risks and zero manufacturing overhead costs; yet every time that product is sold (within your stipulated coverage), part of the profit comes back to you. For emphasis sake, exclusive sales rights allow ONLY you (the agent) to sell a product or service within the market stipulations of your agreement with the manufacturer.

The pioneer of this method is E. Joseph Cossman, hence, it's often referred to as "Cossman Method".

Joe Cossman specialized in securing exclusive *mail-order* (now known as direct response marketing) rights to products already being sold through other channels, and then he would market and sell them through other means using direct marketing and publicity.

Joe had become a multi-millionaire many times over by keying in on profitable but poorly marketed products by their manufacturers. He would ask for exclusive marketing rights to channels of sales the manufacturer had no coverage-perhaps, never even considered as a possible avenue for growth. Using direct mail and publicity, he would turn the product into a market winner.

He had many outstanding successes with several such overlooked products like the Ant Farm, Potato Gun, and the Fly Cake.

WEALTH CREATION NUGGET

Sometimes, the best business ideas are just around us – if you're willing to look closely.

Going through classified ads was one of Cossman's techniques to find interesting products. One day, while reading the classified ads in the newspaper, he saw a little three-line sentence ad that read:

"Send in $1.00 and

We will send you Fly Cake.

It kills flies".

He sent in a dollar and got the product. It was a doughnut shaped solid cake of chemicals that seemed to attract flies and killed them on contact. He discovered the inventor had invented Fly cake as a cheaper and more effective substitute to the sprays used. The Fly cake was long lasting—lasted up to a year. He also discovered something really important—the inventor treated his own invention as an oh-by-the-way-cheaper substitute product. The inventor set up a little factory and he sold Fly Cake only through classified advertisements in newspapers and magazines—and for 25 years, he had only sold about 300,000 Fly Cakes in total!

Cossman found a great invention but with poor marketing! He made the manufacturer an interesting offer; "Give me the exclusive rights for Fly Cakes and I will sell a million pieces in a year, or I will give you back everything I have done with it and it won't cost you a cent," said Cossman.

Joe and the inventor reached an agreement whereby Joe could sell Fly Cakes in any variety of ways he could come up with exempting through Classified Ads. That contract meant millions of dollars to Joe. How? It meant that no one in the world could buy Fly cake unless they bought it from or through him!

He didn't take over the man's factory, he (the inventor) still made Fly Cakes but every sales and order went through Cossman. In a sense, it was as if Cossman had invented the product—all with no overhead cost or manufacturing and tooling costs!

Cossman sold Fly Cake in an incredible variety of ways. Within three years, he had sold over 8 million Fly Cakes (compare that to the inventors 300,000 sales in 25 years). Fly Cake alone made Cossman more than a millionaire - all at no extra cost to him. Cossman went on to repeat the same method successfully with several other products. He proved that his method is proven and can be copied and duplicated successfully for any number of products, at any time, in any given location and by any smart business man.

The prime benefit of having exclusive product rights is the level of control it gives you. If harnessed well (with a winning product), this could possibly be one of the fastest ways to amass great wealth with limited risks at best, and at worst, it still gives you potential for greater income.

Whenever I take a new product to the market, I do everything within my power to eliminate possible future hiccups. Personally, I have only represented – and will only represent – products that I control its sales through exclusive rights or outright private-label (more of this in chapter 6).

EXCLUSIVE RIGHTS VS DISTRIBUTORSHIP AND FRANCHISING

You must understand that exclusive right is not the same as distributorship or franchising. No, it's not. Put simply, with both distributorship and franchising, you would be selling proven products in the market already tested and developed by the manufacturer. You would only be an extra means (probably one of many) for the manufacturer/franchisor to better circulate his products in the market. On the other hand, with exclusive rights, you would be opening up avenues to reach new markets that the manufacturer desires to reach but is not familiar with. Besides, exclusive rights give you total control over your particular niche market and/or geographical location.

With both distributorship and franchising, you can make money but hardly beyond the control of the manufacturer. Besides, they both often require a huge capital outlay in a highly competitive market to begin with. In comparison, securing exclusive rights require minimal capital outlay when planned well and could quite easily become a money spinner in the hands of the articulate entrepreneur. And that's what I hope to achieve in you with this book – wake you up to possibilities that lie right in front of you even with your limited capital.

HOW YOU CAN GAIN CONTROL OF HIGHLY PROFITABLE PRODUCTS IN NIGERIA—AND BEYOND

There's no doubt that times are way more advanced than when Joe Cossman operated. But the facts still remain valid for the articulate entrepreneur. And the whole point of writing this book is to get you thinking and *working* right outside the box!

The secret is to locate a product already selling, but is not available to your niche market yet, or in the case of international rights, not yet available in your country. To many people's surprise, many manufacturers will grant you exclusive rights to a product without requiring you to put up any money.

For example, many companies make great products but don't really know how to sell them or how to locate and reach other untapped markets. The average manufacturer only sells his products in 2 or 3 conventional ways. He sells to a distributor, who sells to wholesalers, who sells to retailers, who in turn retail to the final consumer. His core occupation is manufacturing but, he would like to reach new markets if the opportunity arose—and that's where your expertise comes in.

WEALTH CREATION NUGGET

Ask and you shall get. You can only get
that which you ask for.

Picture this: A Nigerian kitchen utensils manufacturer or supplier who makes all kinds of kitchen utensils; pots, kettles, pans, spoons, non-stick pans, green organic pans e.t.c. The manufacturer only sells through the conventional methods we've just outlined above — that is, from manufacturer to distributor to wholesaler to retailer. Perhaps, he also only advertises infrequently in newspapers and on radio. And basically, that's his business.

Then you come along to the manufacturer or supplier with a proposal and a plan to sell his products through other channels—the internet, your website, newsletters, affiliates, email marketing, through associations, direct marketing, talk-shows or maybe even in nearby African countries. Presenting yourself in a professional and businesslike manner, you ask for one-year exclusive rights to your specified type of distribution, renewable annually for as long as you keep meeting up with your specified sales quota. In this case, propose to have a Performance Agreement. For instance, propose that after one year your agreement specifies you are to have sold a specific number of units and after two years another number and so on. If you meet these sales quotas, you keep your exclusivity. For example, you can propose that you buy at least 1000 units the first year, 2000 units for the next 2 years and at least 5000 units thereafter (I have only quoted figures randomly, do your homework and quote figures accordingly).

You are not requesting for credit or for him to do anything special. You will spread out the first year 1000 units conveniently all through the year and you will pay cash with orders. Well, why would the manufacturer refuse such a proposal? He has the proverbial nothing-to-lose-and-everything-to-gain situation, plus, you would be opening up a new, potentially mass market for him.

If I were a manufacturer, I would snag up this deal – and fast too. Truth is, if you succeed, he would have gained a whole new distribution network in return for his products which was hitherto inaccessible to him. The worst case scenario for him would be if you failed. Too bad though if for some reason you fail but, he would have still succeeded in pulling in some sales through your efforts and at no extra cost or efforts on his part.

Satisfied with the bigger picture you've just painted for him, he realizes he would make more income with much less work on his part.

If you are like most enthusiastic entrepreneurs I know, you'd be all excited to go and secure some business exclusive rights now. But I would advise that you tread with caution though. You don't want to start without the proper legal work in place.

It is wise to work out legally binding exclusivity rights when you decide to build your business selling other people's products especially when you will be introducing the product in a terrain that is new to the product and that you are an expert in. It's not uncommon for manufacturers and suppliers to suddenly "realize" they don't need you anymore after you might have sustainably grown the market and shown them the way to do it without you.

Smart business men and women choose not to labour tirelessly growing some manufacturers' product or brands only to have the sheets pulled right from under them. Instead, they work out exclusives for themselves with hordes of manufacturers worldwide using the argument above. YOU can use this approach as well both locally and internationally to secure for yourself money-making territorial rights to a winning product or products.

STEPS TO REQUEST FOR EXCLUSIVE RIGHTS
1. Find a Selling Product:

The secret here is scarcity and relevance. Do your research and locate a relevant product or brand that is already selling but not available in your niche market. In the case of imported products, your best bet will be to locate relevant product category or relevant product brand that is not yet available in your territory. In selecting a winning product, you must ensure that the product:

i. Is what potential buyers are seeking

ii. Provides solution to a universal problem

iii. Provides a much better way to perform an everyday task or do a common everyday job.

iv. Has a high emotional and/or impulse appeal.

v. Has a high reorder rate.

I personally use a combination of these strategies in selecting winning products for my businesses. My "secret" weapon has always been step V. Many marketers often omit this last requirement but I personally would rather not touch a product without a high re-order rate.

It's a huge plus if you are so fortunate to get such product that matches the criteria I listed above *and* has been sitting on the manufacturer's shelve collecting dust with the manufacturer clueless on how to generate sales – rare to find, but definitely a big plus.

The good thing about a product that is already being sold in a limited market is that the manufacturer already has and can provide you with literature, product samples, and salability of the product has been proven.

2. Approach the manufacturer/supplier intelligently in a professional and businesslike

manner.

If on the international level, often times, professional looking website, emails, and phone calls will suffice. But, if the manufacturer is local and close by and presentations will be in person, you'd better dress the part and project confidence in your presentations. For this, it's advisable that you invest a little sum of money in business letterheads, business cards, envelopes, e.t.c. These days, these things are really cheap to make in small quantities and they prove to be worth it in making you appear efficient and thorough. The manufacturer would want to be represented by a true professional that can perform.

3. Never pay for exclusive rights.

Yes, you read right. Why would you want to pay for

opening up new markets and sales for him when there are more products (globally) looking for people like you than people like you looking for products? If anyone tries to charge you for exclusive rights, please walk away. Remember time is money – and time and your expertise are what you will be providing. Your total upfront cost should basically be for postage, and maybe samples if you can't talk him into giving you free review samples.

Avoid buying and selling inventory before the agreement is signed where you can.

This step is especially true if on the international level. If your intention is to acquire exclusivity rights to a product, then it's against all wisdom to buy and start selling any inventory before the agreement is signed. Some manufacturers will convince you into buying some initial inventory. When you do this, they will likely begin to delay in signing the agreement. Remember that the product you've just taken on yourself to introduce into your market carries their name, logo and contact details fully displayed on it. They know that if the product shows good market potentials in your territory, other prospective buyers/wholesalers will begin to approach them for distributorship of the same product. If their gamble pays off and other prospective wholesalers contact them for business, you could completely lose out. Suddenly, their terms and conditions could change and at best, you would be propositioned to become one of their "distributors" as opposed to the initial plan of being sole exclusive rights owner. Remain focused on your goal before you begin.

4. If you MUST buy an inventory, don't buy a large one upfront.

If possible, just get a few samples and possibly some pictures or catalogue sheets (glossy pictures with product description and specifications) and work with these. There are instances where you will definitely require some inventory to begin with, in such cases, be conservative and start with as little as possible. Use all the selling aids you can get from the manufacturer to start with. (There is even a more clever way to go about it: To test the salability of the product in your own market, try to purchase some inventory but NOT from the manufacturers. Test the market with these first, before approaching the manufacturing company for exclusivity. This way, if they insist on you purchasing a relatively large inventory upfront you'd be certain that you're not investing your funds in an unknown territory.)

5. Don't be afraid to ask for what you want.

Yes, you need to make your offer impressive to the manufacturer to catch his attention, but be careful that you do not overdo it. If you calculate you realistically need to make a certain amount of money per unit and you expect to conservatively sell a specific minimum of units per month, don't be pressured into higher prices or greater sales number. If they propose more than you believe fair or realistic, pass up the product and find another one elsewhere.

6. When negotiating for new products exclusivity right, expect to get your fair share of refusals and turn downs.

Keep working at it though and you will likely get that winner in time.

One of the greatest hindrances to success people battle with every day would be self-limitation. Do not allow self-limitation trick you into believing you can't secure exclusivity rights to a desired product or that manufacturers won't work with you because you're too small or anything like that. You would be selling yourself short if you did. The only way to be certain of how any individual or group of people will respond to your request is to make your best possible argument, under the best possible circumstances.

You owe it to yourself to convince the manufacturer that you are that person that would take his business a notch higher.

A note of warning: Wow him with facts but, don't be too specific or you will give away your trade secrets and he may feel he may not need your services after all.

HOW TO PROTECT YOUR RIGHTS LEGALLY

While it's one thing to secure exclusivity over profitable products, it's another thing to know how to protect your rights. I learnt this the difficult way from a personal experience and you'd be smart if you took a cue from my experience.

The first time I attempted securing an exclusive right from an Indian manufacturer; I simply goofed it up. The manufacturer agreed to pull up a written contract but in my eagerness to get started, I didn't read the fine print. I had ordered my first inventory and had my marketing in place when a lawyer friend pointed out my "goof" in the contract. It turned out that I'd signed a contract which simply stated that I had one-year exclusive and that the manufacturer "could" renew my contract afterwards. In other words, I was to introduce their products into the Nigerian market (largest African market by the way) – and then face the possibility of them licensing the same product line to as many that approached them or worse still, have them kick me out of the picture after the first year. I contacted them to see if they would consider redoing the agreement contract but they refused. What did I do? I sold up my inventory quickly and passed the company for a more cooperative one; this time, I ensured I got it right from the onset.

Experience taught me to always use sales performance requirements as a basis for contract renewal as I explained earlier. If you meet a specified number of units per year, you are protected for your work performed and you retain your exclusivity. This way, both you and the manufacturer are not locked into a long-term unproductive relationship.

By the way, if you are wondering what happened to the Indian company that wanted to rip me off – let's just say that they lost a huge opportunity to have a valid market share in Africa's fastest growing market. They are out.

You may want to have a lawyer assist you in creating a proper agreement, but if you're just starting out and cash is still an issue, a simple contract could be something like this:

EXCLUSIVE SALES AGREEMENT SAMPLE

This AGREEMENT is made on the dates signed below, by and between (your name/company name) of (your address); hereinafter referred to as (your one word name), and (the manufacturer's company name) of (manufacturer's company address); hereinafter referred to as (manufacturer's one-word name); WHEREAS (manufacturer's company) is the manufacturer of (name of product) and is granting exclusive sales rights of said product in Nigeria (or, your niche market); hereinafter referred to as "territory" and WHEREAS (your company) has exclusive sales rights of such products in the above stated "territory";

It is AGREED by the parties above named, in

consideration of the promises and covenants hereinafter contained as follow:

- *(Manufacturer's company) grants to (your company) the exclusive rights to (name the products or brand) throughout the above "territory"*

- *(Your company) agrees to diligently sell and distribute (name the products/brand) in accord with the terms and conditions of this agreement.*

- *(Manufacturer's company) agrees to turn over to (your company) any and all orders and inquiries regarding stated product(s) it shall receive from the "territory"*

- *(Manufacturer's company) will provide (your company) with all technical data regarding the products; sales literature, brochures, catalogues, e.t.c currently in use for the product(s); and any and all future improvements (manufacturer's company)may develop relative to such products.*

- *(Your company) agrees to buy the stated products exclusive from (manufacturer's company) and refrain from marketing similar products in competition with (manufacturer's company).*

- *(Manufacturer's company) agrees to maintain production capacity capable of supplying the orders produced by (your company).*

- *(Your company) agrees to sell a minimum of XXX units (the quantity of products you plan to sell) of (manufacturer's company) products during the first year of this agreement. Should (your company) not sell XXX units within the first year; it shall be to the determination of (manufacturer's company) whether or not this agreement shall be continued for additional years. This agreement shall renew automatically for additional years so long as a minimum of XXX units of the product is sold each year. (Define what one unit of the product is to be)*

- *(Your company) shall have the sole discretion to determine the methods of merchandising the products under this contract (include this clause if you are given exclusive rights to a geographical location)*

- *(Your company) has the unfettered right to, and may, assign its rights and obligations under this agreement to a third party.*

We, the undersigned, agree to the terms and conditions of this agreement on the below-written dates

Signatures

This is only a sample. You can tweak this a little to your own needs or have yours written for you by a lawyer.

I must admit that I don't exactly like and neither do I understand legal lingo that much but, it's absolutely necessary that you have your agreement written and signed.

If there's anything you need to learn early on in business, it is the need for proper documentation. So document and carefully file away everything – just in case you need it.

CHAPTER 6: EXPLOSIVE GROWTH STRATEGY #3: EXPLORE THE GOLDMINE OF PRIVATE-LABEL PRODUCTS.

"When you only sell popular brand products, you build everyone's reputation but your own" - Dan Kennedy

First, let's be clear on what I mean by "private-label". Private-label products are typically those products manufactured by one company (the manufacturer) for offer under another company's (your company) brand. This covers everything from big supermarket chain stores' brand products to small restaurants putting their label on someone else's chili sauce or ice-cream bowl. Put simply, private labeling could be explained to be when a retailer purchases a manufacturers' standard or stock formula and then markets those products under its own local brand.

Essentially, it means you are buying the product(s) from someone else and taking full ownership of that product with your own branding, business logo and all –without research and development cost, without starting from scratch, and without having to deal in huge quantities at a time!

For example, Proctor and Gamble (Giant Corporation) manufactures white detergent powder and sells it under the popular brand name ARIEL. Ariel is marketed and sold via various major distributors, wholesalers, retailers etcetera. A smaller business owner or supermarket owner with good record sales for white detergent powder could purchase similar white detergent powder (from another manufacturer or a private-label manufacturer) and sell as the retailer's brand name. The advantage for a small business owner is this: while ARIEL is targeted to a wider market range, your private label brand is targeted directly to your existent and easily reachable market range and target market niche.

While this concept may still be a relatively novel idea in Nigeria, it accounts for over 30% of all retail sales in grocery stores in both Europe and the USA. In Nigeria, the average Igbo business men are already walking this path, but the full money making potentials of private label products are yet to be tapped.

I know firsthand how profitable it is selling private label products can be— I made my first couple of millions in business selling premium private label products to a highly defined niche market. When done correctly, private label products could very well be your own money making machine.

MEET THE GRAND MASTER OF PRIVATE-LABEL PRODUCTS

Long before David A. Nichols came to Loblaws, a Canadian supermarket chain that was seriously losing money at the time; private label goods were already in existence but were essentially considered as "cheap imitations" of leading known brands.

David Nichols, son of a railway station agent saw underlying opportunities that could be tapped into. First, he discovered that almost all private label lines of food products were of inferior quality (or at least consumers considered them to be inferior quality in comparison with known brands), so only "cheap' consumers reluctantly bought them. He believed the quality of private label products could be dramatically improved and still sell for less than the big brand names because they carry little to zero advertising, distribution and marketing expenses.

Second, he observed that most supermarket chains private label products were unattractively packaged in plain yellow or brown dull and unappealing packaging. He reasoned that in volume, attractive packaging costs just about as much as dull packaging. He raised packaging to levels at par with known name brands and gave bold and compelling names such as "President's Choice" to his products. Nichol's radical change succeeded in giving a "face" and "personality" to products that had been put forward with none.

Thirdly, he discovered that each of the private label products was offered at the lowest price possible, teaching consumers to associate plain packaged private label products with "savings" and "cheap".

Alongside changing the dull packaging to a more attractive one, he also upped the prices accordingly. It still sold for lesser than the higher priced known national brands but was attractive to both wealthy shoppers hot for novelty and, to price-conscious shoppers hungry for value.

No doubt that Nichols' ideas were radical at the time but it paid off. The results of his bold steps were totally outstanding. President' Choice foods (the revamped private label brand) were adopted by over 1,200 stores across the United States and Canada. Nichols increased the private label food sales of Loblaws from about $500 million to over $9 billion dollars in just 3 years!

The success he made with President's Choice was just the beginning – In ten years, he went on to develop more than 1,700 unique products for Loblaws and succeeded in making Loblaws a private-label powerhouse!

As the first and most successful premium private label line, President's Choice amongst other brands has set the tone for a growing number of quality store brands.

WEALTH CREATION NUGGET

There are hidden assets and opportunities around you. Uncover them for profits

---

There are valuable lessons to be learnt from the story of Loblaws' President's Choice.

- Nichols saw a great opportunity in an undervalued "asset" that had been at Loblaws long before his arrival and built on them.

- He focused exclusively on developing house brand products rather than offering them as yet another cheap imitation.

- He delivered comparable quality at substantially lower prices.

- He created a pricing strategy bridge that appealed to both price conscious customers seeking for quality without appearing too cheap and wealthy novelty shoppers eager to try new things.

- He helped Loblaws garner brand loyalty from shoppers

- He drastically reduced Loblaws' store dependence on known brands for sales revenue.

- He saved on marketing and advertising cost by choosing to sell Loblaws private label brand of products through others established distribution networks and stores.

Nichols used President's Choice foods to test and prove that a revamped and attractively packaged private label products sold is a money spinner and his calculated risk paid off.

BENEFITS OF PRIVATE-LABEL TO GROWING BUSINESSES

As much as big companies benefit from private label products, there are ways smaller and growing businesses can also benefit immensely from this.

- No fuss and no manufacturing: This first benefit is really obvious. Why would you want to go through the rigours of manufacturing (factory, machinery, tooling, employees etc) when you can do wholesale buying directly off the press of the manufacturer with your own brand name on the product —especially if you are on a small budget?

- You reap the rewards —same as nationally established brands without the "groundwork" of research and development.

- You reap in substantially higher profit margins than when selling brand name products. You can afford to sell your company's products for less than the known national brands because your products do not carry any brand expense. In other words, your profit calculations do not include the millions of naira that the big companies spend every year on advertising, promotions, product launches and huge employee salaries.

- You have greater flexibility with pricing strategy. You can afford to sell at lower prices in comparison to the nationally established brands for the same reasons I explained in 4 above.

- You have reduced dependence on national brand names for sales

- It helps you create a positive image of yourself for your customers which will lead to stronger customer loyalty

- You are positioned better to succeed in any economy

- It helps you build brand loyalty. After building customer loyalty for months, your customers won't turn around and order the same products from another megastore because they are only available through you!

- Build customer retention: You are offering highly consumable products that will bring your customers back to your store often giving you more opportunities to sell them your primary line.

HOW A SMALL BUSINESS CAN BENEFIT FROM PRIVATE-LABEL PRODUCT OPPORTUNITIES

David Nichols' $500 million - $9billion may be out of reach to you, but aspects of his strategy are still very relevant and well worth considering for a variety of businesses.

Let's say you own a small chain of restaurants or

supermarkets, or fast food joints, or hair beauty salons, or boutiques, or hotels, or car wash, or car sales centre or ... you get the picture. If you develop your own private label line of related products and a terrific proven system for selling them, you can then roll that out to others in similar businesses all over the country (or state first) and create a nationwide sales and distribution organization for your products

In Nigeria and many developing countries, the private label culture is hardly practiced, perhaps due to ignorance of the millions of possibilities therein, uncooperative nature of the existent manufacturing companies, several fixed rules and regulations of several statutory bodies, the absence of outright private label manufacturing companies and many more reasons. There are a host of reasons that the mind can conceive for not venturing into private label business in Nigeria, but even the universe has proven that an Entrepreneurial mind + Creativity + Persistence = Unhindered Breakthroughs.

Remember my private label line of products I talked about earlier? I started that same business from the very comfort of my own house – with no rented office space nor workers. I'd discovered a relatively untapped and viable niche market, aliased myself with a reputable manufacturing company outside the country for the manufacture of same products but with my brand name, logo, theme colour, theme design, a unique selling point and my registered company contact details. I even had my own branded website built for the products. I did my ground work and the manufacturing company was willing to start me off with a low minimum order quantity. The same business has generated some tens of millions in profits for me – and I'd only been retailing it online from my house! Today, I am on the verge of commencing production here in Nigeria for similar product and product line!

To everyone else, the product is mine. Only I know it was private labeled and most importantly, only I know the exact source of my private branded products. This protects your company from business scavengers who have tons of money but will only invest their money in businesses other people (like you and me) have painstakingly grown. They have more capital and resources than you so it's easy for them to order a lot more than you per time and then undersell on price thereby ousting you out of the same business you started. In a sense, an additional benefit of private labeling your products is to protect you from such.

After you might have tested and confirmed the profitability of your private label products, the next step would be to legally protect your brand name by registering the trademark locally. Again, carefully assemble and file away all documents.

It is quite pleasant to work with outright private label companies. These companies are often willing to start you off with relatively smaller quantities. Look elsewhere for production if any company insists on purchasing a large inventory upfront – it goes against my principle of testing the market inexpensively.

I strongly advocate that you test the market first with small quantities before going full steam. Where you can access a Nigerian manufacturer willing to start you off with relatively small quantities at first, please do so. Otherwise, you can easily source your manufacturer from outside the shores of the country with great results.

Often times, I have had many aspiring business men and women consult me to find out the cost of starting and running, and the profitability of certain businesses. They practically want *someone* to do their research for them by telling them manufacturing costs, machinery, tooling, factory, distribution etcetera. Often times after listening to how much experience and resources they have, I had simply redirected them.

Take, for instance, the small business person who has found a niche market for acne treatment and a terrific system for sales – and is trying to get really rich by serving this niche. He could decide to buy from and sell for one of the already existent brand name acne treatment product company –for a low-profit margin. Or, he could decide to OWN and EXPLOIT the business and the niche market out rightly with his own private label brand. He could stake out a leading position as the "#1 Premium Acne Treatment In Nigeria" for his chosen market. And if he is clever enough with his marketing and distribution, any competition that comes in afterwards would have a battle on his hands up surging "The #1 Premium Acne Treatment In Nigeria".

WEALTH CREATION NUGGET

"Invent" a leadership position for your business from the very beginning.

By all indications, he OWNS the acne treatment production company and the only way anyone would know he didn't manufacture and bottled them would be if he told them! If you can get all of these without Research & Development costs, factory machines, fixed overhead, power generation costs and maintenance, why wouldn't you consider the path of private label products first using the minimal capital you have at hand? Or, why wouldn't a smart manufacturer work with you if he knows that by working with you, he has just increased his sales output tremendously and gained massive distribution at no extra cost to him?

The truth is that you can apply and reapply this principle to several small businesses – from the small-scale shoemaker who makes quality sandals and private labels them for your shoe store to the creative hat and bead maker who does the same for your high brow ladies store. From the ice cream maker that makes excellent ice-cream and private label for your fast food joint to the toiletries maker that label specifically for your spa.

Every business has built some level of trust with its customers – leverage this customer loyalty to your favour when introducing your new line of products to your customers. With your terrific way of pushing your products to your customers, your mailing lists etc, guess what brand they will be looking to buy when next they need one – yours! Guess to whom they will go to buy these items every time they need one –you!

Fact: You can get just about any product made or sold anywhere manufactured and private labeled for you in surprisingly small quantities to reap in bounteous profit. Another fact: Applied intelligently, you can exponentially grow your business to great heights even with your minimal capital.

Again, I want to emphasize that for private label, though the manufacturer could still be selling to others, but no one in the world can buy your private labeled brand unless they bought from you – or through your distributors – even though you are not manufacturing it.

That outright ownership and the flexibility you have to fully exploit your product brand for increased profits and growth should be your objective.

WHO CAN BENEFIT FROM PRIVATE LABEL PRODUCTS?

Picture this; You own some retail or online stores, and you spend about N500,000 per year on advertising and on other fixed overhead costs. All your business does is advertising and selling only brand name products. You could spend all that money to generate your customers' interest and then a competitor with lower fixed and recurring costs could become a dealer nearby and short sell on the price – and you're unable to stop him because it's a free market. Not pleasant at all – and certainly not a smart entrepreneur's approach to wealth generation!

A better approach would be to develop your store-owned established private label line of ancillary products to sell to your customers *alongside* other established brand name products. The wisdom in this is simple – you push your own private label products to your customers and gradually build your own products brand loyalty. On the other hand, if your customer is stuck on purchasing only established brand names, you do not lose a sale because you've got them as well.

It is only shortsightedness in business that would get

you questioning if customers would consider buying your unknown brand name. If the story of David Nichols of Loblaws success taught us anything it is that even your relatively small business can pull this off for increased profits with:

1. Attractive product packaging

2. Easily comparative quality to brand names

3. Slightly lower pricing (this is open to debate as some private label brands actually sell at premium prices and they pull it off.)

4. Proven store traffic and patronage and/or online traffic

Many types of retailers, small business owners and even businesses that offer professional services can benefit from selling their own private-label products such as;

- Supermarket stores

- Restaurants

- Hotels

- Bars

- Airlines

- Caterers

- Event Venues

- Hair salons

- Spas

- Cleaning products

- Mass merchants

- Duty-free stores

- E-commerce stores

- Information marketers

The list goes on as far as your imagination permits!

WHERE TO FIND PRODUCTS AND BUSINESS IDEAS

Product and business ideas are really everywhere all around you. Your "manufacturer" may very well be your next door neighbour! I have listed below in no particular order some specific sources that may be of help to you:

- Trade associations

- Association publications

- Trade fairs and exhibitions

- Catalogues

- Directories (usually online)

- Classifieds

- Old advertising

- Import/Export journals

- Business "opportunities sections" in newspapers

- Business "opportunity sections" in online fora

- Advertorials in newspapers

- Product press releases

- Current Events

- Google it already!

CHAPTER 7: EXPLOSIVE GROWTH STRATEGY #4: MAKE YOUR FORTUNE AS A PRIVATE LABELER

"... But the truth of the matter is that just one "toll-position" that is owned by a person can and will make that person extremely successful from a cash money, and also from an asset point of view and forever independent" - Harvey Brody

I had initially considered making this chapter the

appendix to chapter six – but on deeper thought, I decided it deserves a chapter of its own for emphasis.

Leaving it as an addition to chapter six –Explore the goldmine of private labeled products would make many people miss the importance. At best, a mediocre minded entrepreneur would see it as meant only for "giant and established" companies. And that would be an enormous error I certainly wouldn't want you to make. If there's any impact I have worked at with this book, it's to open entrepreneurs to possibilities and ideas they can harness to get their businesses to the next level. Turnaround business ideas that can be used for explosive growth at all scales and sizes of business.

In my early years in business, I founded a hair care product range (you know that already). I'd wanted at a time to expand my range of hair care products. I'd wanted to include pure and cold distilled coconut oil to my product line. Being a relatively new business at the time, I couldn't afford to include the coconut oil line production from scratch. So I decided my best course was to have it private labeled by an existent and excellent source. I found one here in Nigeria and made my proposal directly to the head of management of the company. To my amazement, he bluntly turned down my proposal. He proudly (and ignorantly too – I'll add!) told me they would only sell their bottled coconut oil to me with their bottle, brand and logo boldly embossed on it! In essence, he wanted me to forfeit building my brand and start selling theirs.

From a business consultant's point of view, I can tell you his rigid stance was downright dumb for business. There I was, offering him an entirely new cash revenue source, cash paid up-front, no advertising and marketing cost on his part, no distribution cost and no extra haulage and storage fees, and he chose to remain blind to the enormous business benefit? The smart approach for him would have been to evaluate my proposal and negotiate quantities to order per time. This would have helped him to balance his production expenditures and still pull in a good profit.

On my part, I wasn't up for that. I was only willing to market and advertise my brand (private-labeled, yes – but my brand nonetheless) to my carefully carved out niche market. So I passed up their coconut oil for another source. No problem at all.

GOT GREAT PRODUCT? WHY NOT BE A PRIVATE LABELER?

For many entrepreneurs with great products or product ideas, creating consumer demand, getting lots of customers and building an entire business is beyond their reach and sometimes- it could take forever. But, there's a shortcut. If you produce (or control) a great product, you can private label it for companies, retail shops, small businesses etcetera. These companies already have consumer confidence, advertising, clients reach and most importantly, extensive distribution.

Let's assume you created a revolutionary new kind of dishwashing soap. You might package it one way for Shop-Rite with their theme design, name, logo and identity all over it as "Shoprite's Super Dishwashing Detergent. But, you might also package it in a different sized and shaped container labeled differently for Marbido Stores as "Marbido's Shine All Dishwashing Soap". You can repeat the same for KingsWay Supermarket as "KingsWay O'Clean Dishwashing Soap". And you can continue repackaging it for as many clients as you can proactively get.

One powerful dishwashing formula brilliantly repackaged for many clients and companies. You changed nothing (or at most, you changed fragrance and possibly colour). Instead, you gave your clients a brand that they truly OWN and will enthusiastically sell to their market and through their established distribution outlets.

The idea is not to stick with only the big names in the retail industry – I used big names just for clarity. You can start even with that retail outlet or shop with good patronage close to you.

If you knew the millions it costs most companies every year in marketing and advertising alone, then you'd appreciate the benefits of being a private labeler. You would have succeeded in generating for yourself massive sales through other peoples established distribution and sales network.

It's time for you to remove the bifocals from your eyes and see what results you could achieve with a good dose of private labeling in combination with idea recycling.

Why! Even an information marketer can use a version of private labeling with idea recycling. For example, you could thoroughly research a subject for which people need solutions to, and you could put together an e-book or e-course, alter its packaging and title a little bit, and private label for other e-marketers in the same field. For as many e-marketers in your niche (with their own already dependent mailing list) you could still alter and recycle. Good business for them, great business for you!

HOW EDNA HENNESSEE BECAME A MULTI-MILLIONAIRE THROUGH PRIVATE-LABELING

Edna Hennessee's interest in cosmetics developed after she received a gift of Merle Norman products. She began her career selling Merle Norman cosmetics, but the desire to make her own products fueled her to branch out on her own.

Her experience selling Merle Norman products gave her some leverage in knowing what works and what doesn't. She wrote to various chemical companies, studied everything she could find on chemistry, blending and formulations.

A friend advised her to incorporate aloe vera into her products. At the time, most cosmetic bases were either oil based or water based. The idea of using aloes not only as a part ingredient but as the base for cosmetics was still novel and unsought by the big established companies. She set out mixing up recipes and formulations in her kitchen with aloe as her base.

Her first product was a facial cleanser produced on her kitchen table. Her kitchen served as her first "lab" and the shop and its customers were her testing salon. She could only produce about eight jars worth per time with a handheld blender. Two years later, Edna officially launched her first line of products comprising lotions, creams, and treatments sold in her own store.

Edna perfected her oil base free formulations and consumers loved the results. Her business grew by leaps and bounds. Other executives and marketers wanted in on what made Edna's product lines a success in such short time.

Now comes the interesting part.

Edna knew she was onto something big. She also knew she had to act fast to reap the benefits of her near revolutionary formulations. She hurriedly acquired more lands for aloe vera – you can call it an aloe plantation.

From her experience selling Merle Norman products, she knew that to create national consumer awareness for her products, she would have to be ready to spend hundreds of thousands of dollars (possibly millions) on adverts, celebrity endorsement deals, fancy packaging, TV commercials, billboard, promoters , distribution, etcetera.

She certainly couldn't afford to go head-on in competition against giant cosmetic corporations like Avon, Revlon, and the likes! Edna smartly decided to take another route to massive sales and distribution.

Edna kept her formulas to herself and the only way anyone or company could access her products unique formulations and high quality in-house grown aloe vera was to have them manufactured and packaged for them by Edna herself!

WEALTH CREATION NUGGET

Private labeling is a genius way to get massive distribution fast, with no advertising, and little marketing expense when on a tight budget.

Edna's company works with companies and individuals who wish to develop a product using pure aloe. She and her crew of chemists, graphic designers, farmers and sales associates work with their clients on everything from the formulation of the bottle design and the label on the bottle.

Edna succeeded in building a multi–million dollar enterprise through this simple but profitable process. Her Cosmetics Specialty Labs supplies more than 15,000 private label companies throughout the United States and in over 40 countries worldwide.

GETTING STARTED AS A PRIVATE LABELER

So, how do you get started as a private labeler? The easiest way I know is to just start selling to other local companies and businesses around. Obviously, your existing customer base would be a good place to start.

If you produce high-quality men's leather sandals, then start with local boutiques that sell men's footwear. If you make top-notch hair and beauty care products, start with local beauty supply stores and hairdressing salons.

If you make quality ice cream with a unique flavor, start with fast food joints and eateries. If you are an excellent seamstress or tailor with innovative designs and you can give Giorgio Armani a good run for his money – then by all means approach top rated boutiques and clothing stores!

Once you have a few satisfied private label customers, you can then start a formal "Private Label Program" giving prospective customers examples of what other companies have done.

Trust me on this; many companies (big and small alike) will gladly do business with you if your products are first class and they can have their business brand name on the products – there's this enthusiasm and fervour that comes from seeing your own brand name on finished products.

Do not for a second rule your "kind" of business out of it or think you're not qualified. I have seen private labeling work for as many businesses where a product or products are made. Creatively find a way to include private labeling option to your business for bounteous benefits.

WEALTH CREATION NUGGET

ATTRACT SELLERS – Get others to do your selling for you

To attract private label customers and establish a good relationship with them, you must be sure to make things as easy as possible for them from product concept to package design.

- ✓ Provide a done-it-for-you solution: You should come with a proposal to do all the work for them including the labeling so they just receive the finished product. Your prospective client would be a lot more eager if you saved him undue stress.

- ✓ Don't compromise on product packaging: let's face it; your private label buyer is probably not going to invest much money (if any at all) in marketing. He is likely going to use his shelf space in his store. So potential buyers need to SEE your product and immediately realize its benefit. If you have a consumer product, take the time to package your product so it sells itself. The packaging and design of a product are important if your private-label agreement is with a retailer.

✓ Provide top-notch service: Depending on the type and size of the business, provide marketing support applicably. You can also offer to provide customer service for handling product problems, to take care of product returns, and to suggest product improvements.

✓ Offer Low Minimum Order Quantities: Offer to supply them their private labeled brand at reduced quantities. Do not insist on your private label buyer buying large quantities per time. Do your calculations; know exactly the lowest quantity you need to supply them and still be able to make a reasonable profit and offer them such. Of course, you also need to let them know that the higher the quantity they purchase per time, the lower their cost of purchase will be.

Here, I will advise that you seek a labeling company that allows you offer small quantities to your private label customers and then "gang-run" many jobs together to get a better price for your labels. You can even add your own brand labels to these jobs so your own per-unit label cost will be reduced.

I know it may still just be a dream for many to have their products as the store brands at popular supermarket chains and several retail outlets, but if you don't start out down the private label road, you may never know the potential for your products. If you are completely focused on selling your products under your own brand at wholesale or in retail stores, you may be missing out on a huge growth and money making opportunity.

All over the industrialized world, private labeling has become a lucrative business – you may very well find an untapped oil well down this path!

CHAPTER 8: EXPLOSIVE GROWTH STRATEGY #5 "TWIST" YOUR WAY TO MEGA PROFITS

"There are many ways of taking a product (business), and by giving it a twist you can turn it into a money maker"- Joseph Cossman

---

All over the metropolis of Lagos, you find little roadside bean cake (akara) stalls. The picture usually is that of an unkempt woman bent over, scooping ground beans into her pan of hot oil producing same product as every other woman in her bean ball business – hot rounded bean balls/cakes. If she is lucky, she would make enough money just to get by and run her day-to-day expenses. But, if she's a smart entrepreneur – she could own at least a piece of real estate and a fancy car or two! Nkiru did it.

After having lost her job due to downsizing at her workplace – she worked with an insurance company – Nkiru knew she had to start a business to support her in-and-out of work husband and four kids. She had little capital and decided that any business would do. She settled on the bean cake business but swore to do everything differently from others in the "industry".

Rather than the usual sore sight of an ageing women shabbily dressed while frying and selling the *akara*, Nkiru chose to be smartly and neatly clad with her neat apron, hair covering, and make-up in place. She did the same thing with the two hired hands she got. Her young service girls always had their neat aprons and hair covering on. The great care she took of her appearance, those of the girls and the neatness of her surroundings showed and worked in her favour. But, her greatest winning strategy was just a simple "twist" she added to her *akara* – a circular slice of red bell pepper inserted into a circular slice of green bell pepper visibly placed atop and fried into every *akara* she made. She was also one of the first akara "producers" to serve a rich and spicy sauce to go with her tasty *akara* neatly served in takeaway muffins or perforated foils (– but never in old newspapers!). Customers loved both her *akara* and her entire well packaged "presentation". And sales soared.

In reality, the green and red bell peppers cost little and obviously made little or no significant difference in her overhead production cost, but by totally reinventing the "*akara* industry" by doing something different yet appealing, you might say she found herself in Gold City.

Every entrepreneur at some point should find a way to "reinvent" or "reposition" or "reform" or "re-engineer" or "update" or "improve" (whatever term you fancy) his business or products to a whole new profitable level.

Nkiru made good money from her *akara* business and has since moved onto something bigger.

BEHOLD, MOTHER-IN-LAW PRODUCTS!

In his all time classic, How I Made $1,000,000 In Mail Order (And You Can Too!), E. Joseph Cossman described how someone once brought an unusual product which they couldn't sell. It was a pair of earrings with little bells on them! No matter what they did or how hard they tried marketing them, the products just weren't selling.

Why wouldn't their product work? Was there any way to sell it? Could it still succeed? The manufacturers were pulling their hair out with frustration!

Joe Cossman took the product and gave it a little "twist" (my favourite part of the story). He turned this product into a direct response marketing winner simply by renaming the product "mother-in-law earrings" – this way, you could hear your mother-in-law coming. He targeted wives. It became such a fun earring for wives – both newlywed wives and old wives loved it. ... and thus, turned a failed product into a successful one!

Our homes, offices, closets, refrigerators and garages are full of products that had to be reinvented to succeed. With so much change in the marketplace, some business models and products are simply going extinct.

There are many well-known examples of big-name businesses that have turned their businesses around as a result of reforming or re-inventing their business models including Facebook, Youtube, Apple, Google, Paypal and so many businesses you and I are well acquainted with on a daily basis.

WEALTH CREATION NUGGET

Often, success is just one or two minor adjustments away.

- Apple had great products but didn't become successful until it made downloading of digital music a cheap and simple process with its iPod launch

- In the 1990s, Volkswagens had become a fairly stagnant business, but two of their design engineers had an idea that they thought could revive the company's fortunes. Working secretly and with a secret budget, they re-imagined the legendary Beetle, a car that had been out of production for over a decade. Volkswagen introduced the car in 1998, it was an instant runaway hit, and in the process, reinvented itself as a hip harbinger of retro chic. They have since remained relevant in the car industry.

- Remember when Ankara wax fabric was worn only by elderly women in a two-tier fashion wrapped around their waist? When it was not considered fashionable to wear Ankara? Well, thanks to the modern day fashion designers who reinvented that fashion trend by adding a contemporary touch to their designs. These early designers changed the African fashion scene forever. Now, everyone wears native African fabrics in a million-and-one unimaginable designs and presently hitting the fashion runway in New York, Milan and Paris.

When I started my hair growth treatment business, I had this fabulous hair re-growth product – good quality, great packaging, and proven results. I was sure I could successfully introduce it into the market via major distributors. Well, I thought wrong.

Not one of the distributors would touch my product. I was almost at my wits end when finally one of these distributors pointed out one major problem distributors and retailers had with my product – packaging. It appeared that what I considered being great packaging was "wrong" packaging for the Nigerian market. First, my product was prepared as a lotion – Nigerian consumers were accustomed to hair creams and not lotions. Second, my product was packaged in a narrow plastic bottle with a dropper tip for ease of application – Nigerian consumers were accustomed to plastic jars and would rather dip their fingers in the product to scoop out portions.

It's possible you've got or you've created a product that you passionately believe in but so far, you've been unable to market it regardless of how hard you try. If that's the case with you, then it's time you had a re-think.

Persistence in business is good, but there's a huge

difference between persistence and sheer folly. It benefits neither you nor your business nothing if you keep doing the same thing over and over again and each time you keep getting dismal results. If you have done the same thing over and over again with little or no success to show for it, then it's obviously time to take a different approach.

Get past your sentiments and focus on determining the markets' needs – not what you *think* the market needs – and decide how you can create a marketable "twist" to your product/business to satisfy those needs.

WEALTH CREATION NUGGET

Get rid of ego from your business. It has no business value.

Back to the hair product story: I went back to the drawing board with my new market discovery. Good thing was that I had only ordered a few samples so I wasn't stuck with a large inventory that I couldn't sell. The market was accustomed to hair cream in jars – hair cream in jars I gave them; same product but with a slight adjustment to its packaging. By the way, the adjustment was done by the manufacturers at no extra cost to me. Problem solved.

There comes a time when sinking more money into a failing business isn't going to fix the problem.

But if you can set disappointment, frustrations and ego aside and, with a clear head and fresh eyes, find little but creative ways to reinvent, you can turn losers into winners. That's the Apple story.

APPLE INC: YOU DON'T HAVE TO BE AN INNOVATOR TO BE A SUCCESSFUL RE-INVENTOR

In case you've never heard of Apple, Apple Inc is one of the largest technology companies on the planet. With a market share of about $500 Billion - at the time this book went to print, and still growing –

Apple produces both computer and consumer electronics and is best known for the iPod, iPhone, iPad, and a range of Macintosh computer, notable for their simple and sleek products.

WEALTH CREATION NUGGET

*Realize that people DO judge a book by
its cover*

But Apple had not always been this successful neither

had Apple really been an inventor. Sure, the company did invent the first commercial PC with Apple II- which didn't do too well in the market by the way. But since then, all of Apple's other products have been recreations of existing products.

Apple did not invent the MP3 player; Apple reinvented it (named it iPod) and made it better. Apple did not invent the smart phone; Apple reinvented it (named it iPhone) and made it better. And Apple did not invent the tablet; Apple reinvented it (named it iPad) and made it better... and so on.

Just so you know, Apple was a floundering company on the brink of bankruptcy but, it managed to charter an unparallel path to success in information and digital age. So much so, it's become one of the world's largest companies and the world's largest technology company.

There are many contributing factors to Apples' success but I find worth mentioning the intriguing "twists" that took Apple Inc from an average company to becoming an enormous winner:

Product Appearance: Apple is often referred to as a design leader with first class design in all its products so they stand out from their competitor's products. Their design philosophy is based on minimalism. They remove all the clutter both from the products outward appearance and the interface.

Positioning: "If you can't be first in a category, set up a category you can be first in" – advertising experts Al Ries and Jack Trout. Apple has positioned itself to be a lifestyle product for wealthy people, innovators and people with good jobs and great taste. It became a desired product brand but not easily affordable. When people can afford to buy Apple products they do not haggle about price, the price would be secondary and the image of having an Apple product would be more important. This exclusive premium positioning is what Apple sought for and created from the onset and it has helped set Apple aside from competitors.

Focused products: Simple and easy to use. There were MP3 players before the iPod and smart phones before the iPhones, but Apple's innovation was to distill those products down to their fundamental purposes. For example, "1000 songs in your pocket" used to promote their first generation iPod, thus avoiding confusing and overburdened products. The result is their customers know what to expect from Apple and they usually get it.

Visionary sacrifice: Given the popularity of the iPod and its centrality to Apple's bottom line, Apple should have been the last company on the planet to try to build something whose explicit purpose was to kill music playing devices. Yet, Apple's inner circle knew that one day, a phone maker would solve the interface problem, creating a universal device that could make calls, play music and videos, and do everything else too – a device that would totally destroy the iPod. Apple's only chance at warding off that threat was to manufacture the iPod killer itself – the iPhone. The iPhone is one of the most successful products of all time and has pulled in billions of dollars for the company in revenue. Now, that's innovation that builds a business.

Hype: When Apples' competitors go one way, Apple heads in the opposite direction. While Apples' competitors promoted their products based on functionality and even pricing; Apple centered its promotion strategy around creating hype. Apples' marketing team excels in creating mystique and excitement long before the launch of all Apple products. Their theatrical style and panache style amongst other things succeeded in making Apple products a to-aspire-for and a must have for millions of consumers and "fan boys".

WEALTH CREATION NUGGET

Borrow, reuse and reapply ideas

In reality, there never has been anything that was totally revolutionary about most of Apples' products. Yet, it has grown to become the world's largest and most successful technology company.

Apple gets incredible results following an already well

known and proven system; take a concept already developed by others, sometimes even already considered to be exhausted and "twist" it a new light.

There really is no set formula for reinventing your business but often, success is just one or two minor adjustments away. Many people give up just one tweak away from converting experimentation and struggle to victory. You know your industry and market as good as anyone and should realize when to draw the line between persistence and sheer stubbornness.

WEALTH CREATION NUGGET

You are responsible for the success or failure of your business ideas.

Blaming the marketplace, the customers, those in

charge of distribution for not seeing how great and awesome and needed your product is cannot possibly lead to success. It may be comforting, but it is self-defeating and even childish.

If Apple had gotten mad at their market after the invention of their first commercial PC Apple II and had gone home, it'd be just one more failed digital technology company among thousands that also failed. Instead, they kept seeking different and better ways to present their products in a way that the public would respond to.

SACHET "PURE" WATER INDUSTRY: A REINVENTION STORY TO THE TUNE OF OVER NGN1 TRILLION IN NIGERIA.

Do you recall in the 1980s and early 1990s when bottled drinking water was somewhat considered a luxury for the affluent in Nigeria? As a growing child, I remember there were only two major popular brands: Ragolis Table Water and Swan Natural Spring Table Water.

At that time, quenching your thirst while on the go was usually done with "ice water" – water manually filled and tied in transparent polyethylene bags. Hygienic? Well, who cared about hygiene when thirsty and a cheap substitute to the luxury brands was easily within reach and affordable? All that changed when a visionary young man introduced treated and machine packed water in sachets.

WEALTH CREATION NUGGET

Gap fillers are money makers

George Ekeh saw a gaping hole in the drinking water

business. Most people couldn't afford the luxury brands every time they got thirsty, neither did they really like buying "ice water" because of hygiene concerns.

George figured that consumers would gladly pay just a tiny fraction of the amount they spent on luxury brand bottled water to buy equally well treated and machine packed water in sachets. He also figured that consumers who bought "ice water" (the larger market share) would readily pay a slightly higher price for sachet water to quench both their thirst and their hygiene concerns. George figured right.

Not too long ago, the Director-General of the National Agency for Food And Drugs Control (NAFDAC), Dr. Paul Orhii made it public that sachet water sales across the country generate an estimate of NGN 7 billion in sales daily!

Although George Ekeh quit the drinking water business early on in the game, his smart thinking reinvention of the entire industry generates billions across Nigeria, provides employment for many Nigerians, and of course, drastically reduced the epidemic of water-borne diseases across the nation. Quite a twist I'd say!

STRATEGY CHECKLIST FOR GIVING YOUR BUSINESS AND PRODUCTS A NEW, INTERESTING AND MARKETABLE TWIST

One of the views that I fervently argue is that it is easier to reinvent something by adding a marketable twist to it than it is to invent afresh altogether. For example, when Apple Inc (Yeah, Apple again – I identify with success all the time – you should too!) picks an existing category, they take a product with a ***proven*** large market with ***pre-existing*** demands and take it to entirely new levels of design and user friendliness.

If you seek explosive growth and success in your brand new or existing business – regardless of the size of your business – do what Apple does: take a popular everyday product category and then provide answers to these questions where applicable to your business.

How can I:

- Make it look better?
- Make it taste better?
- Make it smell better?
- Make it sound better?
- Make it fit better?
- Make it last longer?
- Make it function better?
- Make it more useful?
- Make it more exciting?

- Make it more interesting?

- Make it more fun?

- Make it less cumbersome?

- Make it save more time?

- Make it more cost friendly?

- Sell it as a premium?

- Solve a current problem with it?

- Provide extra value with it?

- Adapt it for a new market? Etcetera.

Below is a quick list of some of the strategies you NEED to consider each time you (re)create a product, service, business or marketing campaign for quicker sales, massive sustainable growth ... and wealth.

RESIZING

Make It Smaller: Is there something that is successful big that could be just as successful small?

Apple phones and computers are mega-slim gadgets. Consider the slim phone, iPad mini, minivan, extra slim sanitary pads, the cupcakes, spices in single-use sachets, etcetera. Jik bleach and Hydrozone bleach were household brands but suddenly on the market scene arrived Hypo bleach in smaller packs and in single-use sachets.

Make It Bigger: Is there something that is successful small that could be just as successful big?

Big screen TVs and home Theatres, Jumbo sized noodles, big size coke bottles. Nigerian Pepsi "long-throat" bottle etcetera.

Add To It: Add some "special" agent for example skin lotion enriched with anti-ageing vitamin E, table salt with iodine and vitamin A, products with video *and* transcripts *and* CDs *and* available online, E-Books + extra bonuses.

Subtract From It: Paraben and sulfate free products are beauty products sold on what has been removed from them. Online banking and banks – takes away building, branches, tellers and long queues (thankfully!). A "stripped" down version of a product to offer as a last resort in information marketing. Foods with no preservatives. Gluten-free, Lite-free, fat-free, and sugar-free foods. Tubeless and wireless product and so on.

REPOSITIONING

If your product or service seems to be a fading trend, consider repositioning. For decades, Lucozade was marketed and sold as an aid for recovering from an illness. It was only recently re-positioned as adult fitness drink to tap into the booming fitness trend amongst adults. Lucozade Sport became a phenomenal success as a leading sport and energy drink.

A pharmaceutical company almost stopped the production of a cold medicine because they couldn't correct the drowsiness it caused. Someone aptly renamed it Nyquil and re-positioned it as a bedtime cold medicine. Nyquil suddenly became the largest cold selling medicine in the market at the time.

REPACKAGE

Loblaws' sales grew astronomically by re-packing their plain private- label products with snazzy attractive packaging. Consider changing and upgrading the look of your packaging materials to suit the market needs and trend.

Information marketers make a killing by repacking and selling the same information as PDF document, CDs, DVDs, Webinars (web seminars), live seminars and even hard copy print books. The extra savvy information marketer will even go further as to repackage his products for other marketers in a related niche to sell to their own mailing list.

RENAMING

Did you know that 7UP was originally named Bib-Label Lemon Lime Water (*say what now?*) and was initially marketed as a means of settling infant's upset stomach?

When author Bob Morrison self-published his book, it went on sale as "The Entrepreneur's Manual" – it only sold 12 copies. Disillusioned by these sales, he renamed his book Why S.O.Bs Succeed and Nice Guys Fail In Business. The book has since sold over 1 Million copies!

Almighty Google was initially named Backrub – I'd sooner Google a topic than "Backrub" it.

Remember the all-time bestseller book Men Are From Mars, Women Are From Venus? Author John Grey didn't get much attention with his first title "What Your Mother Couldn't Tell You and What Your Father Didn't Know. He shortened and renamed it, the rest, as they say, is – well, over 50 million copies sold!

ADAPTATION

I like to call this the intuitive Copy-Cat system. If it works in one business, will it work in mine? If it works in one geographical location, can I make it work in mine?

What **proven** business **system** can I copy and adapt from one type of business to mine? What proven business growth system can I adapt from one geographical location?

Mainstream e-commerce stores such as Amazon, Aliexpress, Ebay have always been popular in western countries. Nigeria's Jumia and Konga have shown that it can also work here – and many more local businesses are trailing the same path already.

For example, I opted not to publish and market this book the traditional route. I adapted the semi self-publishing and marketing strategies taught by my mentors from the US. And if you've got this book in your hands, then it proves my "copied" strategy is successful.

SPECIFIC SOLUTIONS

Waterproof, wear-proof, tear-proof mascara and lipstick are best-selling cosmetics of all time. Spanx allows women mask their figure imperfections. The pet door lets your dog in and out of the house at will without you letting him in and out and without compromising your home security. The non-stick cooking utensils prevent burning.

RECOMBINE

A common example is the combined supermarket-gas station-convenience store-fast food joints. Another one is the combined spa-wellness store-barbing salon-hairdressing salon-games centre. 2 in 1 shampoo – combined shampoo and conditioner.

TIME FRAMES

Do It Faster: Some years ago, Indomie noodles wowed the nation with its "3-minute Noodles" promotion. SlimFast had a very successful ad campaign based on the theme "Give us One Week and We'll Take Off The Weight". Today, several beauty products race of the shelves with claims such as "Visible results in 7 Days" boldly written on the package.

GENERAL PURPOSE VS SPECIAL PURPOSE

Compare the general purpose body bathing soap suitable for all skin types with the special purpose soap for sensitive, oily and dry skin. Several companies in the home-cleaning product industry have different specialty products for every conceivable purpose. There are grease stain removers, oil stain removers, carpet stain removers, tiles stain remover and so on. In reality, about 80% of the products are 95% the same; the most significant differences are their labels and the specific niche they were created to serve.

EXAGGERATION

Years ago, Pearl Cream sold millions of its products by

delivering this guarantee in TV commercials: "If your friends don't actually accuse you of having had a facelift, return the unused portion for a full refund". Even I have used a version of this for one of my recent hair loss treatment advert online: "If your friends don't actually question if you've had a hair transplant, come back for a full refund". Cheeky right? But it works!

In a commercial, Ariel detergent demonstrated that it could remove the toughest combination of oil, grease and grime from a white garment leaving it absolutely spotless in just a single wash. All these are nothing more than *satisfaction guarantee* but with much more impact by being demonstrated with exaggeration. No one believes they will be accused of having had a facelift after using Pearl Cream and neither does anyone believe Ariel would remove the toughest combination of stain and grime from clothes in a single almost effortless wash, but the exaggerated promotion instantly drives the message home and *enforces* the mind to want to reckon with the product and brand.

This strategy checklist is by no means conclusive. There are endless of ways to reinvent your business. It's your duty to brainstorm, research, plan and most importantly **execute** ways to add profitable twists to your new or existent business for maximum profits.

CHAPTER 9: EXPLOSIVE GROWTH STRATEGY #6: CAN A FORTUNE STILL BE MADE IN A SERVICE PROVIDER BUSINESS?

"If instead of working on making more money, the average business man would spend an hour each day in quiet contemplation of how to be of greater and more creative service to his clientele, he and they would be richer for it" - Earl Nightingale

75% of all the new jobs created in companies globally are in the service category. Why? Because those are the businesses expanding most consistently and rapidly. 75% of all self-starter entrepreneurs are also in the service category. Why? Because they often do not require a huge capital to start, do not necessarily need acquisition of special university degrees and is often a lot easier to start.

When most people think of service businesses, they automatically think small.

The guy who fixes your faulty refrigerator. The solo operator plumber who comes around to repair broken water pipes or at best, the guy who runs a "business center".

I've got news for you – the service business is booming with many giant businesses and blue chip companies as members.

AMAZING! WHAT $100 – AND A BIT OF
INGENUITY CAN DO!

United Parcel Services UPS is one of the largest logistics and delivery companies in the world. The company delivers over 15 million packages each day to over 6 million customers across the globe. But, it wasn't always that way.

There was a time many years ago that UPS was just the vision of two "ordinary" young men.

WEALTH CREATION NUGGET

Find a way to become the bridge
between a demand and its supply

---

19 years old Jim Casey and 18 years old Claude Ryan observed the difficulties companies and individuals encounter in delivering telegrams (most people didn't

own phones then) and parcels from one place to another. With their opportunity antennae tuned to the right frequency, they figured that if they could offer the service of delivering parcels and messages to the recipient intact and within the shortest time frame possible, they 'd have a viable venture on their hands. The young lads followed their business intuition.

Jim and Claude got together to form a small messenger company known as the American Messenger Company. In 1907, they formed their new unlikely business venture. And they did by borrowing $100 —and 1 bicycle shared between them.

Sending telegram was a frequent thing and it had to be hand delivered. In the beginning, they primarily delivered these telegrams but eventually expanded into transporting pretty much anything that could be transported on a bicycle or on foot.

Soon after, these two enterprising young men had a thriving business on their hands. In 1919, the company officially changed its name to United Parcel Service UPS.

UPS, as we know it today, is one of the world's largest package delivery companies. It operates in more than 220 countries and territories around the world. Its delivery operations use a fleet of more than 100,000 motor vehicles and 500 plus aircraft.

No one can say whether Jim Casey and Claude Ryan ever imagined that their small messenger company which they began over 100 years ago would become such a global icon. But, by providing simple cost and time-saving services to companies and individuals alike, by making their company the bridge between a demand and its supply, the company these two young men created with a $100 loan from a friend became an over 50 million dollar business.

ONE MAN'S JUNK IS ANOTHER MAN'S PROFIT ... MILLIONS ACTUALLY!

At 18 years old, Brian Scudamore was at crossroads. He was preparing for college but he didn't have the funds to pay for his education. One day, while eating a meal at a local McDonalds, Scudamore started racking his brain, desperate to come up with a plan to raise funds for his tuition, when suddenly he saw an opportunity that would change his life forever. "It was then that a beat-up, old truck that advertised Mark's Hauling rumbled through the drive- through," Brian says. He thought he could do better than that so he decided right then and there to spend his remaining $700 in savings on purchasing a used pickup truck to haul junk away for a fee. He called his new business "The Rubbish Boys" later to be smartly named 1-800-GOT-JUNK?

At first, Brian took to alleys and streets looking for people in need of his trash removal services. The need for his service became very apparent. Two years after Brian started his trash removal service, he reached the point where he needed to invest in new equipment and hire helpers. Brian's business was so successful that his opportunity costs were weighing heavily on him. He decided not to finish his last year of college - to the dismay of his father, who was a respected liver transplant surgeon whose wish was for his son to become a doctor too.

The North American franchise has expanded to over

325 locations. What Brian started as a $700 investment in an old truck has become one of the fastest growing franchises with a fleet of over 1000 trucks and revenue more than $100 million.

WEALTH CREATION NUGGET

Perhaps your first (next) million could be in transforming an underserved and often neglected industry.

Trash is Brian's treasure. In his words "I am proud to take an industry that was very beat-up and transform it." Brian's company has been successful because junk is a universal problem. "Not everyone has a truck or the time to remove their own trash. It can be a difficult task to find someone who will haul off all your unwanted junk."

Brian's idea to take a fragmented and dirty business and clean it up was strategic. He did everything differently from the norm in the junk removal business. From his one truck, he added clean, shiny trucks that act as mobile billboards, neat and friendly uniformed drivers, on-time service and upfront rates. Finally, he mixed in a culture that is young, fun and completely focused on solid, profitable growth. His change from the old-beat-up-truck kind of business set a new standard for trash removal.

Brian's 1800-GOT-JUNK? drivers call their customers 15-30 minutes before a scheduled pick-up to confirm their appointments. Then to ensure consistent, continued service, Brian's company calls their clients to follow up after each job to the amazement of customers who were used to uninterested waste removal companies who do the job halfheartedly, take the money and leave.

WEALTH CREATION NUGGET

Create a powerful vision in your mind
– then ACT on it.

Much of the company's early success can be attributed to Brian's young ambition. With a vision of creating the "FedEx of junk removal, he made the future of his business happen first in his mind and then actively worked on making his vision a reality.

You will remember that is business idea was sparked off by "Mark's Hauling Truck"? Well, I do not hear a "Mark's Hauling" making the news today – perhaps, it's even gone out of business – same as many other service provider businesses whereas 1 -800-GOT-JUNK? has pulled in over $100 million in revenue. The difference between Brian's "little" used truck trash removal business and most other service provider business is in his vision – he created a vision in his mind, looked beyond all the dirt, *creatively* worked out how to achieve his vision and then *proactively* went about its establishment.

What about his doctor father that wanted him to become a doctor? He's become a major fan of his son now. And his friends and colleagues who most likely scoffed at his "dirty" business idea? I am certain that they probably toe a path to Brian's door now or perhaps, even have to schedule appointments weeks ahead to see their friend or at the least – they proudly declare "Sure, the 1-800-GOT-JUNK? guy is my pal."

The big questions for you are: How many times have you been at the receiving end of poor and inadequate service? How many times have you thought to yourself "I am sure I can do a lot better than that"? How many times have you looked beyond just complaining to thinking of how you can create better service and then build a business of it?

Perhaps your first (next) million and several millions after that could be in transforming an underserved and often overlooked or left for- government-to-tackle industry.

At present in Nigeria, several arms of government both at the state and federal levels are doing their best to get rid of trash safely and are partnering with the private sector in Nigeria to achieve that goal. My mind beats to think of what the likes of visionary Brian would do with such an opportunity.

WHO CAN SELL A SERVICE?

The answer is simple – anyone and everyone. We all have skills, knowledge, and even experiences that people are willing to pay for in the form of a service; or are willing to pay you to teach them your specific skill or knowledge. Selling services actually know no boundaries.

What skills do you have that people will gladly pay you for? Any skills you possess can be your best and by far your most marketable asset.

Everyone has one or more skills people are prepared to pay for in terms of a service provided to them, or to learn. Unfortunately, most people have a tendency to underestimate the true value of their skill sets and experiences. Remember that, what comes naturally to you may not come so naturally to others and therefore, it becomes a marketable asset.

You might "think" your particular knowledge or expertise may be of little value, but if someone else needs or wants to learn about that knowledge, It's very valuable to them – and they will pay you – the expert for it.

If you know how to plan and throw one heck of a party, people will pay you as their event and party planner. If you are great with kids and start a daycare service; people will pay you for taking care of their little ones. If you know how to write original articles; people will pay you as a freelance or in-house writer. If you know how to sell products and services online, people will pay you as an online marketing consultant. If you know how to write and post engaging and relevant posts on social media, people will pay you as their company's social media image maker. If you are skilled at connecting people to needed resources and you love to help businesses grow, people will pay you for your referral and networking services. If you have particular skill sets that help people start up the business of their dreams, people will pay you for your coaching and/or consulting services.

WEALTH CREATION NUGGET

Use resources you already have at
your disposal

Odds are that if you have the skill, you probably also have the tools and resources you need to start at hand.

Using existing resources saves you money and time. Start with whatever you have and expand later as the business grows.

Just about any talent and skills sets can be turned into a profitable service business.

IMAGINE MAKING A FORTUNE WITH YOUR HOBBY!

If you are serious about creating a highly promotable service, but with no ideas for that service, you might want to take a new look at your own hobbies and personal interests. Tara did.

Everyone has talents – and by tapping into what you do best, you could carve out for yourself a very comfortable living. Successful entrepreneurs all over the world understand that the entrepreneurial route is laden with a lot of obstacles and uncertainties. It is infinitely easier to stick with something you are passionately interested in long enough to get successful than to set out to get rich in whatever seems like the best opportunity of the moment.

Many people achieve great success by making a living from their interest and hobbies – stand-up comedians, musicians and lots more. And many more people can and should look to their hobbies and personal interests as the source of inspiration for establishing their business.

HOW AN HOBBY-TURNED-SERVICE BECAME BIG BUSINESS

While waiting to be admitted into the university, Tara Fela–Durotoye worked for a make-up outfit and there she totally mastered the art of make-up. Soon after, she gained admission to the University to study law. Much as she concentrated on her studies, she still always had time to do her friends and colleagues make-up as a hobby in her spare time.

After seeing the transforming effect of her make-up touch on people's faces and receiving varied compliments on her work (which she did for free at the time), she decided to get her first professional make-up kit.

In 1997 while still an undergraduate Tara founded her first business as a Bridal Make-Up artist with her first make-up shop. With a start-up capital as low as N15,000 and a passion for the art of make-up, she began her conquest of the make-up business world in Nigeria.

Obviously, not every hobby can be turned into a

profitable venture – I mean if your hobby is sitting around all day in front of the TV with the TV remote control in one hand and a can of beer in the other – I do not see how you can make any money out of that.

To determine whether your hobby can be built into a sustainable business, you must first ask if you have a great service that people want and will **pay** you for. Do people want it? Does it save people time or cost? Does it proffer a unique and better way of doing things? Bottom-line: you must be able to easily demonstrate and prove its marketability. Tara's testing was at the University.

HOW CAN YOU TURN YOUR HOBBY AND PASSIONS INTO MONEY?

There are many ways you can turn your hobby and passions into a profitable business. Tara started out by offering her makeup services to clients. She diversified into selling Tara private-labeled (I detailed private-label in chapter 6 and 7) beauty products. And later into coaching and consulting services to people who want to learn her secrets. Now, she has devised a way to pass on what she knows for immense profits – and built an impressive business empire too while at it – that's where I'm headed here.

There are some hobbies, interests and passions we all have but take for granted. There are so many "services" you and I mistakenly offer for free that could fetch us money. Recall that initially Tara offered her make-up services for free before deciding to make money from it?

What is that thing you love doing and do so well that people seek you out for? Have you thought that with clever "packaging" you can offer the same service for a fee? I can almost bet you that all the stand-up comedians and musicians you see today offered their services for free at first before they were "discovered" – in other words – professionally packaged.

Yours might not be a service that can be packaged and sold outright, but what if your hobby and passion are what others would like to learn? What if people will pay you to learn what you know and do so naturally that you've taken it for granted?

WEALTH CREATION STRATEGY

What you know and take for granted could be of immense value to others. Find ways to package and price your knowledge and expertise for huge benefits.

Let's say you love doing crafty things like sewing, or making jewelry, or making hats or exquisite hair braiding. You could be an excellent cook with innovative and delicious recipes. Perhaps your hobby and passion are throwing a heck of a successful party or you could be an expert at rearing livestock profitably ... just about any useful hobby and personal interest you have.

You may not be able to sell your service directly BUT, you could devise ways to product-ize your service. You could put together a "how-to" guide, make videos demonstrating techniques, or even put together idea books, for starters. You can put together an introductory product or a product that takes people through the stages of creating a project from beginning to end at different skill levels from beginner to advanced. I am talking information marketing here.

Briefly, information marketing is taking the knowledge you have and packaging it up in a way that others will pay you money to get it.

Look around you. What do you think is the greatest thing people need? Solutions. Knowledge. Information.

Information marketing is a phenomenal business. It allows you—no matter what your background, experience or education level — to achieve financial and personal freedom very quickly, from scratch and with limited resources. Seriously, I have seen and know people who built an entire business and amassed a great fortune as information marketers.

What's more, *you can do it using what you already know*.

By leveraging what you already know and creating an information marketing product, you can add an additional stream of income to your existing business. Even better, many information marketers soon discover that they can make more and have greater freedom with their information marketing products than they can with their regular business or jobs.

Besides the money you make from this, there are several other great things about creating an information marketing service business.

- You can do it in your spare time.
- You can start small.
- It doesn't cost much to get started.
- It can provide a consistent, steady "money while you sleep" stream of income.
- It won't feel like work because you'll be talking about something you love and have a vast knowledge of.

To get started: Pick a hobby or passion, something you love to do in your spare time (it must be something that can be monetized), or a skill you've picked up along the way. As mentioned earlier, there are unlimited possibilities for this.

Think about what it is you love to do? Garden? Travel? Cook? Make-up? Health and fitness? Marketing? Cosmetics formulations? Make something out of Wood? Golf? Blogging? Take care of your pet?

Successful parenting? Fertility lessons? Finance expert?

Once you've picked a topic, you'll want to do some research to see if there is a good market for it. You would also want to research a profitable angle to appeal to your target market. After you've done some research to determine there is a market and interest in your topic, then all that's left is to combine your passion with a successful information marketing strategy.

Just about any talent and skills sets can be turned into a profitable service business.

I won't be able to teach you comprehensively about starting an information business based on your passion and interests here in this book. But I can assure you that learning how to "package" and sell your information to a focused niche market could be one of the most empowering things you do for your business.

HOW "ORDINARY" PEOPLE TURNED "ORDINARY" SERVICE BUSINESSES INTO MILLIONS

I often hear this lament from people "If only I had more capital, I would...". I must admit that in my early days as an aspiring entrepreneur, I had at several times vented in a similar way and had fallen prey to devising "brilliant" business plans that required huge capital outlay. And of course, I never was able to raise the capital needed. I didn't have the prerequisite requirements to get a loan from the banks and finance bodies considered it too risky to finance a newbie at a business with such huge amount. It didn't matter that my business plans were well researched and properly presented.

In retrospect, not starting my business with a loan

from any finance body was for the best. When you start your business as a newbie, regardless of how well researched it might be, there's always a learning curve, and sometimes these curves are so steep that there are bound to be mistakes and oversights in your calculations. Why make these mistakes on borrowed money with legal implications?

Sure, I am a big proponent of big dreams – and I also believe in trying to reach your dreams at the highest level possible – why crawl when you have the opportunity to fly, right? Big dreams and the audacity to dare to reach them help to keep the zeal for success and achievement alive, but, you must plan to start with the resources that are readily accessible to you. There's always a way to get started where you are and with what you have; you just have to be motivated enough to start it and start it NOW.

Success stories abound of people who started with only a little capital – plus a good dose of faith and gumption.

TRANSPERFECT TRANSLATIONS INTERNATIONAL INC.

TransPerfect is one of the five largest service companies in the world with estimated revenues around $300 million. The company employs about 300 full-time staffers, over 4,000 subcontractors, with over 31 offices in about 30 countries in 6 continents of the world. Despite the success of the business, TransPerfect had humble beginnings.

Having once worked for a translation company after getting her Bachelor of Arts degree in Modern Languages and Literatures, Elizabeth Elting knew that the translation industry was composed of various small outfits offering inconsistent quality.

She was then a student studying for her MBA when together with her classmate Phil Shawe, they knew that huge opportunities await them in the translation business. They founded and formed TransPerfect in 1992 – wait for it – in their college dormitory rooms!

Their road to success was not easy as the early days of TransPerfect were run on the tightest shoestring budget.

In Elizabeth's own words:

> *"We basically started with zero money. We didn't even have a computer. We rented one for $40 a month. We had no office space, no employees.*

We used a credit card loan for a few thousand dollars but that was it. And the moment a check came in, we would run to the bank so we could pay our linguists. Our first goal was to be in an affordable office in six months – which we did. After a year and a half, we hired our first employee, and two years later we moved into the office complex we are in now. Then we started opening offices around the world. In the beginning, we hired subcontractors and focused on quality control by hiring an outside translator, editor, and proofreader for each project. In the beginning, we took a very aggressive approach to sales. We took it one client at a time and one project at a time."

After years of toiling, Liz and Paul blended together their passion for languages, culture, and business to achieve their goal of transforming their translation business to becoming one of the premier companies in the industry. The results are beyond remarkable.

WHAT MIGHT YOU ACHIEVE WITH YOUR INTUITIONS?

Coming up with winning business concepts need not be a brain-whacking exercise. There is one simple formula that works every time: - Combine a **need** with something you love doing.

David Marcks never thought that chasing geese as a way to keep his hyperactive dog busy could become a lucrative business.

GEESE POLICE: A REAL LIFE HOME BUSINESS SUCCESS STORY

23 year old David was working as a golf course superintendent. He had problems with over 600 geese residing on the golf course. He and other golf superintendents tried several approaches to keep the geese off their golf course: from geese repellent

chemicals that don't always work, to streamers or other "goose frightening" props that altered the appearance of the golf course. Killing or injuring the birds was out of the question.

After trying various approaches unsuccessfully, he stumbled on the idea that he could perhaps train his dog – a Border Collie – to drive off the geese. He contacted the American Border Collie Association and told them what he wanted to train his dog to do and they thought he was a lunatic.

David's insane idea worked. Within weeks, David didn't have any geese on his golf course – but all the neighbouring golf courses suffered greatly because all the geese went someplace else.

With the geese gone, however, a new problem popped

up. David had a new problem: what will he do with his hyperactive dog that could get destructive if not kept busy?

What David did next laid the ground for Geese Police. He offered the services of his dog to herd away the geese in neighbouring golf courses with no charges just to keep his dog busy.

Word about David and his dog started to spread among other golf course operators. David intuitively saw this as a terrific money-making opportunity.

While Geese Police started in the golf course sector, golf courses are now just about only 5% of his business now. The majority of his business, about 90% are corporate parks and playgrounds – corporate and township properties.

Today geese police incorporated – worth over $10 million – has remained in the forefront of the industry that it pioneered. With over 50 trucks and 70 dogs, Geese police now have franchise offices in virtually all over the US.

WEALTH CREATION STRATEGY

So yours is not truly a service industry? Find a way to include service – and clobber your competition with service.

GRAY KLOTTING

In chapter 4 of this book, I wrote about 3 young men who toed the path of their past experience and set up their own clothing line Gray Klotting.

What I find remarkable about their venture is that they started out with nothing but past experience in combination with zeal and determination – and they started when all three of them were just undergraduates in their first year at the university. Of course, being full – time students they ran their business only part-time.

The singular unique thing about them is that knowing that they had no stable workshop while in school and they couldn't be everywhere at all times, they mastered their business so much so that you only had to send them your regular US cloth sizing and they would make for you an exact sized tailored-to-fit African-themed outfit and deliver right back to you in any location in Nigeria. Amazing how they do it so accurately, but this singular extra service has garnered so much patronage for their young business over the years.

At the time of editing this book, they are all youth corps members with the National Youth Service Corporation (NYSC) for the mandatory one year of service to the country after graduation. All three of them are determined to follow their chosen line of business upon completion of the mandatory service year with plans to have each of them manage an outlet in at least three major cities in Nigeria.

WEALTH CREATION NUGGET

*Sell maximum convenience at
minimum hassle*

With their unique way of saving you the time of having to come for measuring and fitting and added value service of delivery of finished products, I believe we will still hear more of these enterprising young men and someday, we will be celebrating Gray Klottings.

The key factor that fuels any service business today in any geographical location on the planet today is getting a solid business idea and finding ways to revolutionize it by simply thinking outside the box. Think service – think WOW!

CHAPTER 10: **TAKE YOUR SMALL BUSINESS TO THE NEXT LEVEL!!!**

It's very likely that in your current business or in the business that you about to create, there is room for explosive growth. Here are a few tips for recognizing and exploiting your growth avenue.

THINK BIGGER!

Most big businesses began as small businesses. You can expand, duplicate, diversify, combine, add more products to your existent product line etcetera and turn your small business into an excitingly growing business.

THINK BROADLY!

Stop defining your business too narrowly. Give yourself

mental creative room to maneuver and to respond to new growth opportunities.

THINK SERVICE!

Even if your business is not exactly a service business, find creative and *useful* ways to include service components in your business – your customers will love you for this.

THINK LEVERAGE!

What is your greatest asset? Is it a loyal and highly responsive clientele? A trusted brand? A remarkable sales strategy? Is it store or website traffic? A phenomenal location? Unique products? Exceptional service? Outstanding guarantees? A large and targeted mailing list? Vast market knowledge? Whatever it is, ask yourself how you can get more leverage from it. How can you better exploit it for bigger business? Ask yourself, in how many more ways can you make more money from the same business you already have or from the same skill set you possess already.

Popular Nigerian blogger Linda Ikeji leverages her blog lindaikejisblog.com in many ways to generate more income. She generates income from regular paid adverts, her affiliation with Google ads, sponsored posts among other sources of revenue. Same blog, same work input but diverse ways to generate income.

I have studied a young and thriving Nigerian internet marketer Joe Okoro use his extensive skill of driving targeted online traffic to his websites to build an enviable business in various niches ranging from fitness to health issues to information marketing and even network marketing.

Ben 10 was a cartoon character, of use originally only in short cartoons for kids. But, that same asset has been leveraged by its creators via comic books, movies, apparels, toys, bags, theme parks and so on.

Almost every child (and adults) in Nigeria know and love their Indomie noodles. Indomie has found ways to leverage their success in the noodles category (which kids love) to other product categories for kids as well.

I leveraged on the words Indian, ayurvedic and hair re-growth to grow my hair care business.

THINK SYNERGY

Synergy simply means the combined effect of two or more things working together in order to create something that is *bigger* or *greater* than the sum of their individual efforts.

What elements can you combine under your single roof or umbrella that *multiply* your revenue rather than just add to the value of your business?

Uzo owns and runs a brick-and-mortar store plumbing and building materials supply business. To leverage, first, he took his business online by creating a website www.armitagewares.com where people can place orders and get it delivered. Plumbing and building materials could be quite cumbersome and in some cases fragile to move. Uzo included supply and delivery right to your doorstep in his business. Next, he observed that clients still complain about poor plumbing installations. He introduced the service sector where a client can easily have his new purchase installed by his experts. He also started selling his own brand – not manufactured by him but private-labeled for his business (Chapter 6).

With his private-labeled brand, he has not only garnered brand loyalty from his customers, but also market relevance as he now also sells his private-labeled brands to sellers – distributors and retailers.

WHAT NEXT? TIME TO EVALUATE

Throughout this book, I have written about the successes of and strategies used by other successful entrepreneurs to grow their businesses. Some of these are big and well-known businesses; others, on the other hand, are corporations or individuals making a fortune in relative anonymity – but making a fortune nevertheless.

For all these successes I have shared, there are many more businesses that have failed. Even I had more than a fair share of failure at the start of my entrepreneurial journey.

Yes, Nigeria is going through a difficult growth phase. Yes, we are currently faced with diverse economic growth problems that every developing country faces as a price for growth. But even in the midst of these "growth phase challenges" lies many untapped opportunities.

The fearful see only obstacles but the bold and gutsy entrepreneur sees untapped opportunities.

Why else do you think foreigners still troop to do business here regardless of all the odds? Or why do you think manufacturers globally seek to get their products recognized and sold in the Nigerian market? I'll tell you why. It's because they see the myriad of explosive growth opportunities that lie untapped right under our noses!

It will be rather unfortunate if you read this book with a ready-made skeptic mindset quickly dumping ideas that do not immediately seem directly and specifically relevant to your particular business. A big mistake.

If you've gone through this book quickly saying "that doesn't apply to my kind of business" or "that certainly won't work here in Nigeria", then, I will send you all the way back to Chapter 2 – Developing A Winning Mindset – so you can change your perspective.

It is my hope that through ***Business Big Time: Secret Strategies To Explosively Grow Your Business Even If You Start Small***, you realize you don't have to be born a "genius" for your business to succeed neither do you need to have a fat bank account, godfathers, college degrees or even " a totally unique and never-thought-of-before" idea. It often only takes an idea –your own money-making idea and what you choose to do with it.

The lazy-minded keep giving excuses and waiting for the perfect situation and condition to start; the daring and gutsy entrepreneur starts now – and then steadily grows his way to "perfection".

A FINAL WORD FROM THE AUTHOR

If you found valuable the explosive growth tips in this book, would you mind taking a minute to write a review on Facebook? Even a short review will help, and it will mean a lot to me and to many seeking avenues of growth in their business. The link is www.facebook.com/DilimOkeke

If someone you care about is struggling with starting and growing a business especially if the person's resources are minimal. Please send him the link to this book both online and paperback.

If you'd like to order copies of this book for your friend, company, school or group of friends, please go to www.DilimOkeke.com

Finally, if you'd like to get free bonus materials and receive updates on tested, proven and duplicable business growth strategy updates, you can sign up for my newsletter at www.DilimOkeke.com

Start now! Start big! Start confident! Grow explosively! And God's speed!

MY PERSONAL DEVELOPMENT QUOTES

"If opportunity doesn't knock, build a door." – Milton Berle

"I had to make my own living and my own opportunity! But I made it! Don't sit down and wait for the opportunities to come. Get up and make them." – Madam C.J Walker

"All disruption and trauma in the marketplace births new opportunity, and those on the alert for it and who act on it can enjoy incredible experiences and success." – Dan Kennedy

"Always bear in mind that your own resolution to succeed is more important than any other." – Abraham

Lincoln

"Do more than is required. What is the distance between someone who achieves their goals consistently and those who spend their lives and careers merely following? The extra mile!" – Gary Ryan Blair

"If you take responsibility for yourself, you will develop a hunger to accomplish your dreams." – Les Brown

"I have always made a total effort, even when the odds seemed against me. I never quit trying. I never felt that I didn't have a chance to win." – Arnold Palmer

"Don't tell me the sky is the limit when I know there are footprints on the moon" – Paul Brandt

"We become what we think about most" – Earl Nightingale

"If you don't go after what you want, you will never have it. If you don't ask, the answer is always no. if you don't step forward, you're always in the same place." – Nora Roberts

"The only way of discovering the limits of the possible is to venture a little way past them .....into the impossible." – Arthur .C. Clarke

"Desire is the key to motivation, but it's the determination and commitment to an unrelenting pursuit of your goal – a commitment to excellence – that will enable you to attain the success you seek." – Mario Andretti

"Success is the sum of small efforts, repeated day in and day out." – Robert Collier

"It is better to aim at perfection and miss it than to aim at imperfection and hit it." – Thomas Watson

"Expect the best. Prepare for the worst. Capitalize on what comes." – Zig Ziglar

"The only limits are those of vision." – James Broughton

"Don't ever let someone tell you, you can't do something. Not even me. You got a dream, you got to protect it. People can't do something themselves, they want to tell you, you can't do it. You want something, go get it. Period. All right." – The Pursuit of Happyness

"The winners in this life think constantly in terms of I can, I will, and I am. Losers, on the other hand, concentrate their thoughts on what they should have or would have done, or what they can't do." – Dennis Waitley

"Every great dream begins with a dreamer. Always remember, you have within you the strength, the patience, and the passion to reach for the stars to change the world." – Harriet Tubman

"If you always do what you've always done, you will always get what you've always got." – Henry Ford

"Until you're ready to look foolish, you'll never have the possibility of being great." – Cher

The question isn't who is going to let me; it's who's going to stop me." – Ayn Rand

"Ambition is the path to success. Persistence is the vehicle you arrive in." – Bill Bradley

"Don't spend so much time trying to chose the perfect opportunity, that you miss the right opportunity." – Michael Dell

"Be a generous giver and an excellent receiver." – Anon

Most people give up just when they are about to achieve success. They quit on the one-yard line. They give up at the last minute of the game one foot from a winning touchdown." – Ross Perot

"Formal education will make you a living; self-education will make you a fortune." – Jim Rohn

"I celebrate myself and sing myself." – Walt Whitman

"Dream on it. Let your mind take you to places you would like to go, and then think about it and plan it and celebrate the possibilities. And don't listen to anyone who doesn't know how to dream." – Liza Minnelli

"Don't limit yourself. Many people limit themselves to what they think they can do. You can go as far as your mind lets you. What you believe, remember you can achieve." – Mary Kay Ash

"Losers believe in luck ......Winners believe in the correlation between cause and effect." – Anon

"Things work out best for those make the best of how things work out." – John Wooden

"The person who makes a success of living is the one who sees his goal steadily and aims for it unswervingly. That is dedication." – Cecil .B. DeMill

"Don't worry about impressing people; just get busy inspiring them." – Anon

"There are no secrets to success. It is the result of preparation, hard work, and learning from failure." – Collin Powell

"Poverty is when large efforts produce small results.

Wealth is when small efforts produce large results." – David George

"If you believe you can or believe you can't – you're right." – Henry Ford

"If your expectations of success are strong, they will generate the motivation you need to act, to do whatever it takes to succeed." – Dilim Okeke

"Unless you try to do something beyond what you have already mastered, you will never grow." – Ralph Waldo Emerson

"Real obstacles don't take you in circles. They can be overcome. Invented ones are like a maze." – Barbara Sher

"I can't change the direction of the wind but I can adjust my sails to always reach my destination." – Jimmy Dean

"To be independent of public opinion is the first formal condition of achieving anything great." – G. W. F. Hegel

"When the bull's eye becomes as big in your mind as an elephant, you are sure to hit it." – Alejandro Jodorowsky

"Being defeated is often only a temporary condition. Giving up is what makes it permanent." – Marilyn Vos Savan

"He who is not courageous enough to take risks will accomplish nothing in life" – Mohammed Ali

"There is one quality which one must possess to win, and that is definiteness of purpose." – Napoleon Hill

FREE RESOURCES TO GROW YOUR BUSINESS FAST!

Would you like free access to time-tested and evergreen business strategies that can grow your business? Would you like to do business like the big names we hear and celebrate today – even with limited capital? How would you like to receive profit-making strategies detailed to geometrically improve your business both offline and online? Sign up for the Big Time Business newsletter – practical growth lessons exclusive for our members only.

For FREE access, subscribe at www.DilimOkeke.com NOW!

www.ingramcontent.com/pod-product-compliance
Lightning Source LLC
Chambersburg PA
CBHW021422170526
45164CB00001B/50